THE YOU FACTOR

BARLOW

Barlow Book Publishing Inc.
77 Douglas Crescent
Toronto, Ontario
Canada M4W2E6

Library and Archives Canada Cataloguing in Publication data available upon request.

book   ISBN 978-0-9917411-1-3
ebook   ISBN 978-0-9917411-2-0

Printed in Canada

To purchase copies please contact:

Sarah Scott
Publisher
Barlow Book Publishing Inc.
77 Douglas Crescent
Toronto, Ontario
Canada M4W 2E6

For more information, visit **www.barlowbookpublishing.com**.

THE YOU FACTOR

A HANDBOOK FOR POWERFUL LIVING

LESLIE STRONG

BARLOW

*I would like to dedicate this book to
all women who want to live a life
full of joy, fulfillment, and power.*

CONTENTS

Introduction

You are probably picking this book up because you are looking for something. You may not even know what. You just realize that parts of your life are not working. You may even look at all the components and think, *I have the partner, the house, the kids, the job, the vacations, and the friends. It looks good. But then why don't I feel so great?* You aren't really happy or fulfilled, not the way you thought you would be or should be.

You may be wondering if you should change something—your job, your partner, your neighbourhood—or whether you should just grin and bear it. But then the thought of sticking it out has you thinking, *Really? I still have 30, 40, 50 years left. Can I continue living this way for that long?*

If you find yourself in this unfortunate place, the first thing to realize is that you are not alone. Recent articles in *Time*, the *Huffington Post*, and the *American Economic Journal* have reported that unhappiness in women has increased in the past 40 years. In fact, 75% of women now claim to be unhappy.

But it didn't take news reports about rising unhappiness to tell *me* that many people were having a tough time feeling good about their lives. First in my work as a gender specialist, then in my career as an executive coach, I've heard plenty of stories. And most of them centre on frustrations and dissatisfaction—with jobs, family, relationships, and work–life balance.

And I've had my own experience with the unhappiness that bubbles up in life despite all of the good.

So what's going on here? Why the epidemic of unhappiness?

My work and my personal experiences have led me to the conclusion that the prime cause of most of our current unhappiness can be boiled down to something I call "The YOU Factor." Or to be more exact, the absence of "The YOU Factor" in our lives. If you are unhappy, it's likely because you have given up your personal power. You no longer feel in control of your life. You feel other people or outside circumstances are calling the shots. You have, in a sense, given up on *you*.

But the good news is that there is a way to remedy this, to find happiness, to regain joy and satisfaction. And it is as simple—and as challenging—as adopting a different way of thinking. What it takes is an open mind and willingness to look at your life in a whole new way. It takes a commitment to change *you*, but it only takes you!

What makes me so certain that "The YOU Factor" works? Well, because I've tried it myself.

Not long after I started my own business, GenderMark, a consulting firm specializing in marketing to women, I got married and had children. I had always wanted to stay home and raise my kids. I wanted them to have a parent around at all times. I figured being a stay-at-home mom would be so much easier than running my own business that I would be excruciatingly happy. As it turned out, I did not enjoy staying home—at all. I loved my kids, but hated the other parts of the job, like the laundry, and the cleaning, and the groceries, and *the everything else*. Even doing some contract work didn't alleviate my frustration and boredom. My only solace, apart from the adorable kids that I had brought into the world, was to see my girlfriends, drink lots of lattes or wine, and dump all the complaints about my sorry sad life onto their laps.

One day I had had enough. Scrolling through the Internet, I found a website for an executive coaching program. Only then did I pull my ostrich head out of the sand. How ironic that my own life had become so dysfunctional and frustrating when, during my contract work as a life coach, I was helping others with very much the same thing. Reading about the training program for executive coaches, I realized I had a choice. I could continue to be a hostage of my central vacuum cleaner and hate every minute of it, or I could take the leap, go back to school, and start my life as a career woman again. Suddenly I was thinking up all kinds of creative ideas to make family and life work while I was going to school. All of a sudden, I had lots of options.

Although the workload to make it all happen increased, I still kept my commitment to the "no nanny" philosophy. I chose to work while my kids were at school and in the evenings once they were in bed. I got someone to clean once a week and a sitter once a week, so I could still go out for wine with my girlfriends. I dropped the lattes, worked a lot harder, and got a lot happier. Although it was a lot to juggle, I could live with it, even with the stuff I didn't like, because I was happier overall.

It wasn't an answer for everything in my life, of course. More than once, I headed straight for the pitfalls, and stumbled badly. But while I was changing my own life and coaching others, I had developed a number of concepts and techniques to regain control and freedom and joy in life. Although these weren't a recipe for instant gratification (some may take time), whenever bad things happened or I made mistakes, I felt better right away, knowing that I could use these powerful tools whenever I needed them to get my life back on track. And because I got a lot better at recognizing the traps, I got a lot quicker at climbing out of them. Finally, I decided I should be sharing what I learned more widely with others.

In *The YOU Factor*, I show you how to regain power and control over your life. I discuss how to look at yourself, your personal values, and the stories you tell yourself about life to determine how you are really feeling. Then I explain how you lost that power in the first place, and why you might feel stuck where you are, with no way out. I share concepts and techniques that will help put "The YOU Factor" back in your life—giving you control, regaining your power, and discovering all your options and choices. And I warn you about the traps out there—the thinking and habits that can derail your happiness and thwart your efforts to change. *The YOU Factor*'s 10 power tools, as well as its easy-to-follow exercises, tips, and advice, will help you to move forward and make important, meaningful changes. They will help you get into action, overcoming past unhappiness, frustrations, complaints, and bitterness. And they will help you change the way you think about yourself, your choices, and life's challenges.

I promise you—you can create a life that you will love. So let's get started!

Happiness is not a goal; it is a by-product of a life well-lived.
—Eleanor Roosevelt

1

How Are You?

How are you? How many times a day are you asked that question? How often do you really stop and think about *how you are?* Like most people you probably just automatically answer "Fine thanks." I'm asking you honestly to consider how you are. Are you okay? Are you fine? Are you great? How are you, really? Take a moment to think about this. Look at your life right now, or just one part of it, like your career or your home life.

In my coaching practice, I often ask my clients to rate the different parts of their life on a scale of 1 to 10. I ask them to look over the many dimensions of their life—their marriage, children, work, friends, fitness level, and overall joy. They usually end up with a rating of 6 out of 10—a rating equivalent to "I'm fine thanks."

Is that you? It's not bad. It's a pass. But is 6 out of 10 the kind of life you really want to lead? Is that what you wanted when you graduated from university, when you started your career and got married? Probably not. You hoped for a 10 out of 10. But now is your enjoyment of some parts of your life slipping? Maybe it's something simple and annoying, like that 20 pounds you've gained since you turned 40. It could be your home life; your marriage isn't as exciting or fulfilling any more. It could be your job; you're phoning it in, and you're just doing it to pay the mortgage.

So how *are* you? Why *do* I ask my clients to rate their life? I ask because it's important to assess where you are now. It's important to find out, so you can have a clear picture of where you're losing ground. This slippage or dissatisfaction can happen slowly, over many years, and if you're like me, you might not realize what has been happening. So you need to be honest as you answer the questions that follow. Then you'll see whether you've slipped, and if so, how far.

What Fills You Up?

What fills you up? That question comes from a personal advisor, the entrepreneur and venture capitalist David Folk, who created The NEXT Program, a revolutionary neuroscience-based program for struggling couples and families. And it's one that I now employ in my coaching practice. What fills you up? What gives you the greatest joy, makes you feel glad to be alive?

A fill-me-up is an experience that leaves you with a positive feeling for an extended period of time, like a day. It leaves you with a sense of power and strength to take on the work in your life and to give to others, with patience, support, understanding, love, kindness, and generosity.

One of my fill-me-ups is having deep, meaningful conversations with certain friends. I always feel differently after a lunch or a visit when I've engaged in an open and authentic dialogue where I learn something, or make a difference in some way. Another one for me is going for a run or getting in a really hard workout. I love the feeling of having pushed my body to its limits.

A fill-me-up could be completely different for you. It could be the joy of learning a new skill, or creating something—an idea or a business. It might be the fulfillment of helping someone improve his performance or live more effectively with chronic pain. It could be the joy of achievement—winning a big award for your work or making a huge profit.

Perhaps it's helping your child understand fractions or having a bonding moment with your spouse. You might be filled up by managing a staff, which allows you to have an impact on your organization or your world. Or it could be the simple pleasure of enjoying the outdoors, in the garden or at the top of a mountain in winter. There are many ways you might fill yourself up, so write them all down.

Exercise: Did you fill up?

Think about your day. Did you fill up? Did you do anything to make you feel that joy you remember in those great times?

What about this week? Did you fill up? If you say no, you have plenty of company. Most people do not do one thing in their day that actually makes them feel really happy, satisfied, or worthy. Some people go days, weeks, years, or even a lifetime without creating times that fill them up.

Exercise: Identifying activities that make you happy.

Ask yourself, "What do I like?" What aspects of your day make you happy? What do you love about your job? What do you like or love about your friends, family, hobbies? What is going on in your life that you enjoy or don't enjoy? Why? What fills you up?

There is no right or wrong, good or bad. What makes you happy is what makes you happy; it doesn't matter what others think. After you've made your list, rate the items from 1 to 3 (1 being the most important).

This is what my list looks like:

What fills me up?	Rating	Time needed
Reading non-fiction books	3	1 x week
Seeing friends	1	1 x week
My kids	1	daily
Spending time with my spouse	2	3 x week
Laughing	1	5 x week
Shopping	3	2 x month
Learning	2	1 x week
Working out/being active	1	daily
Eating healthy	1	daily

A blank form to use for your own fill-me-ups is found in the Appendix, on page 147.

Next, think about how you can incorporate the fill-me-ups into your day. Then add those into your calendar. The 1s go in at least twice a week, 2s at least once a week, and 3s at least once or twice a month.

At the end of the week, keep a tally of your fill-me-up completions. How often did you do each one? Finally, record how you felt having incorporated these practices into your week.

What Drains You of Energy and Joy?

What did you do today that did not fill you up or make you feel happy and satisfied? How many times did you sigh and complain to yourself about your job, your family, your life in general? All too often, we do what we think others want us to do or what we think we have to do. But it's not what we want to do. For example, I don't like putting the groceries away. Silly but it seriously makes me unhappy and a little stressed.

Sometimes we can eliminate these "drains" from our lives. When my children got old enough, I had them put the groceries away. But some drains you can't delegate or get rid of. You can, however, make them less unpleasant by surrounding them with fill-me-ups. If I can't wait for the kids to put the groceries away, I promise to reward myself by doing something I enjoy when I'm done with the chore, so at least I end up with a good feeling. You can also plan to do the unpleasant task after you've had a fill-up moment, so it won't feel so bad.

Exercise: Minding the drain.

Make a list of everything you really dislike doing in your day. Rank them from 1 to 3, 1 being the tasks you hate the most. This is what my list looks like:

What drains me?	Rating	Time allotment
Laundry	1	1 x week
Grocery shopping	3	3–4 x week
Cleaning	1	daily
Putting things away	2	daily
Managing challenging relationships	3	1 x month
Tidying up	1	daily
Picking up after my kids	2	daily
Returning emails	3	daily

A blank form to use for your own drains is found in the Appendix, on page 147.

Can you eliminate the drainers from your day? How? If you can't eliminate or delegate the drainers, what can you do to make them affect your mood and your day less? What other activities can you build in around them to make them feel less arduous or annoying?

Next, add how often you need to do each drain in the "time allotment" column, so you can see how much of your day, week, or month is spent on the drains. This will make you more aware of the number of fill-me-ups you will need to balance those tasks.

Comparing the fill-me-up table and the drain table will give you an idea of what your week will look like. Use the fill-me-up table to create a list of what to do to balance the bad with the good. While I'm returning emails, for example, I will send a note to a friend after every five emails.

Personal Values: You Know What You Want, but What Do You Need?

We've talked about what "fills you up," the activities or experiences that make you happy and fulfilled in the short term. But you also need to look at the larger, more profound areas that you need to be happy, contented, balanced, and satisfied with your life. These are what really make you tick—I call them "your personal values."

"Personal values" are different from fill-me-ups and different from the broadest meaning of values. How? Fill-me-ups are the day-to-day activities that put a smile on your face, fill up your heart, or give you the energy to move forward. "Values," in its most common sense, usually refers to concepts that may have moral or ethical connotations or to ideals that people aspire to. So when asked about their "values," people will often say things like "honesty," "hard work," "being a good friend," "family," "my faith." Rather than personal values, however, I call these sorts of things "aspirational values." Likewise, a company may have a set of values for the employees to keep in mind as they conduct business day to day. In this case, values provide a context for behaviour. A family may also have values that provide the framework for parenting or for ways the parents would like to have their kids behave. In our house, we have our family values—words such as "fun," "adventure," "health," and "excellence"—on the kitchen wall. These are essentially the framework that influences our family vacations, sports, and meal times.

But when I refer to "personal values," what I want people to get at is the truth of what makes them tick. These may not be things that you would see as ideals or goals of any sort, but they are things you need to make your life work for you. They are the fundamental drivers that determine who you are. They give you energy and provide you with a sense of balance and of being on the right path. When your life is not in line with your values, the opposite occurs. You feel as if you are struggling, unhappy, frustrated, and life is hard.

But it is sometimes difficult to know what these personal values really are. As we grow up, our family, our peers, and our community influence what we think of as our values. But are these things what we really need in our lives or are they just things we think we should have?

Here's an example: Your parents are both accountants. All your life they insisted that this was the right path for you too. You studied hard, and while you didn't really enjoy the courses, you stuck to them diligently, knowing that accounting was a good career. When you graduate, your job as an accountant has you working largely by yourself. You realize that day after day you are not happy in your position: you feel drained, unmotivated, and frustrated. These feelings flow over into your social life, leaving you with no desire to touch base with friends or enjoy a balanced life.

But if you looked at your personal values honestly, you would acknowledge that you are an extrovert. You love conversations, connectedness, collaboration, creativity, and freedom. Yet, every day, for 10 hours a day, none of these personal values are present. This is what drains you. You have a job that is not in line with those ways of being that make you tick, energize you, give context to who you are. Living out of balance with your personal values is what is making you miserable.

But how do you figure out what your true personal values are? Try the exercises below to find some answers.

Exercise: Identifying personal values through peak experiences.

Write down three peak experiences in your life. They can be anything, but they should be specific—not a week or a season. These experiences should represent moments when everything in your life seemed fantastic. You were happy, on top of the world, empowered. You truly felt like "this is the place I am supposed to be." A good place to start is your fill-me-ups. Review them to ascertain what you love to do. If you look deep into these fill-ups, you will find some of your values. For example, a fill-me-up for me is to see my girlfriends. That is the action, but what is it that my girlfriends fulfill? They fulfill my need for connectedness, and connectedness is one of my values.

After writing down those moments, or your fill-me-ups, think about the qualities or factors involved in the experience that made it so ideal for you. What was it about the things you were doing that made the time feel so wonderful for you? (Take a look at the sidebar "Possible Personal Values" if you need some help.) Write them down. Do you have a few values that showed up on more than one of your experiences? If so, circle those. Now take a look at the values that you noted only once. Be honest with yourself. Are they really you, or are they values that you would like to have or were brought up to think were important? If you determine that any of these are not truly in line with who you are, cross them out. Ideally you should have five or six values remaining in your list.

Possible Personal Values

Balance

Beauty

Commitment

Connection with others

Control

Cooperation

Creativity

Excellence

Excitement

Fairness

Financial security

Flexibility

Freedom

Health

Humour/fun

Independence

Justice

Knowledge

Leading

Learning

Making a contribution

Nature

Organization, structure

Passion

Peace

Perseverance

Planful

Precision

Predictability

Problem solving

Recognition

Results

Risk

Risk averse

Rules

Security

Self-expression

Self-improvement

Serenity

Solitude

Spontaneity

Status

Structure

Success

Teaching

Teamwork

Trust

Varied work

There are many more!

Exercise: Identifying personal values through negative experiences.

Another way to see what your personal values are is to examine times when you were clearly not happy. This might be a moment of extreme frustration, or a time when you felt angry and annoyed. It could be a specific argument—or the issues you tend to argue about. It could be experiences that made you feel vulnerable, lost, uncertain, or out of balance. Write three or four of these down. Now try to identify what exactly pushed your buttons. What was present (check the Personal Values sidebar for help if necessary) that made this such a negative experience for you? Once you have a list, try to identify the value that is missing or that might be the opposite of the concept you have recorded. For example, if you have a miserable time working on a group project, perhaps it was the collaboration and consultation process that got under your skin, suggesting that "independence" might be one of your personal values. Add these personal values to your list.

Using Your Personal Values

While we might be able to identify the things that make us tick, we often forget our personal values when we make an important choice in our work or private lives. It's easy to overlook them. You go for the big job or the serious payout even though it means working with a huge team when you really feel best operating independently. You buy into the fancy lifestyle, with the ski chalet and the lakeside cottage, even though you love, above all, the spirit of freedom and spontaneity, something hard to get when you are managing three houses and the transportation in between. The key to leading a happy, fulfilling life, then, is aligning our personal values with our choices as often as we can.

So far, we've looked at what fills you up on a day-to-day basis and what you need over the long term to be happy and fulfilled. You might find there is a gap between what you do and what makes you happy, at least in some parts of your life. If you have spotted a gap, this is a good thing. If you can see that you did not fill yourself up today or this week, and your decisions did not correspond with your long-term needs, you have actually taken the first step.

If you can see that gap, you can do something about it. Take, for example, a client who came to me because she felt her life was in constant imbalance. She was self-employed but kept thinking she should go to work for a company so she'd be safe and taken care of. As we ran through a couple of her peak experiences and her negative "buttons," we discovered that one of her values was security. Once she realized that this value was fuelling her desire to give up being self-employed, we could also see that it conflicted with many of her other personal values that were in line with being her own boss. Now she knows that her need for security may cause her some discomfort, but that she has to take into account the positive things she is getting by sacrificing a little security. And she can decide where the balance should lie between these things and whether or not changes might improve a situation.

Exercise: Identifying the gaps.

Think of what makes you happy. What do you love to do? If you could do anything with your day, what are some of the things you would incorporate?

In one column, write down your list of personal values or needs—in other words, what makes you feel fulfilled.

In a second column, write down all the things you did during the week.

Now try to connect each action with an appropriate value. For example, the values I would place in the first column are adventure, connectedness, and freedom. Over the course of the week, I paid the bills, did some chores, and had five coaching sessions.

So I would draw a line from "connectedness" to my five coaching sessions. Nothing else for me matched up. Therefore, my week was obviously a little out of line with my values. I'm okay with this because I'm aware of my values, and most of the time I do manage to insert plenty of them, creating a balanced week. For most people, however, every week of the year would look this unbalanced. This is how we become human "doings" instead of human beings.

This chart shows whether my personal values and my actions were aligned. It's just an example—your list may be much longer.

Personal value	Aligned or gap	What I did this week
Adventure		Paid the bills
Connectedness	——————————	Had five coaching sessions
Freedom		Chores

A blank form to use for your own values and actions is found in the Appendix, on page 148.

How often did one of your activities connect with one of your personal values?

How can you design your day or your week so your needs, or at least some of them, are met?

Now think about a choice you made in the past year. Look at your list of personal values. Did the choice you made connect with one of the personal values on your list?

Are You Stuck?

It's one thing to notice that you haven't filled up in a while, or that a lot of things you do in your day drain you of energy and joy. Doing something about it is an entirely different matter. In this part of your self-assessment, it's time to check whether you have the ability to change if you don't like the way things are going. If you can't, or you feel you can't, you're stuck.

Exercise: Are you stuck?

Ask yourself these questions:

> Am I angry or frustrated?
> Am I unhappy but don't know why?
> Are there people or circumstances in my life that drain me of energy?
> Do I feel unloved, unappreciated, or undervalued?
> Have I been complaining about the same thing for more than a year?
> Do I feel like I'm spinning my wheels?
> Do I feel trapped, and I can't get out?
> Am I having a hard time making a decision, and I don't know which
> way to turn?

If the answer to any of these questions is yes, you're probably stuck. You can ask these questions about different parts of your life, by the way. You might be stuck in some parts of your life, but not in others.

2

Where Did My Power Go?

Is It Them—Or You?

If you feel stuck, if you feel that you have lost joy and fulfillment in at least part of your life, there is a way out. The first step on this journey is to look at who is causing things to happen in your life. Who's the main actor, the protagonist? Is it them—or you?

It sounds like a simple question, but it's easy to lose sight of who is the main actor in your story.

Here's an easy example. The teenage son of one of my clients was given a used car to drive around the suburb where he lived. It was a gold four-door sedan, not a very cool car for a teenager, only one step away from a van. One day while he was trying to park at a mall parking lot, he nicked the fender. He quickly called his father. "What happened?" his father asked. "It wasn't my fault!" the teen cried. "This car is crap! You gave me a crappy car!"

He was blaming the fender-bender on his four-door sedan, and his parents for giving him a crappy car, not his own inability to park in a crowded lot! Now that's pretty obvious, but we do this more than you might think.

For example, one of my clients had felt powerless and unhappy in her job for many years. She was unable to do what she felt was right for her clients because her boss was a micro-manager and overturned her decisions at every step. And she wasn't able to be creative in her role because her boss stomped on all her ideas. What's more, her motivation had drained away as her boss wouldn't let her do her work in her own way. Now, I'm not saying that any of these complaints were invalid, but what I noticed right away was that the main player in my client's story seemed to be the boss, not her.

Sometimes my clients tell me that there are a host of other people who keep them stuck. They are the women who feel they have to do it all. They believe that if they don't do it, it won't get done, or not the way it needs to be done. They do everything for their kids and husband at home, and for their co-workers at the office. Even if they and their husbands both work, they bear the brunt of the household too. They say if they don't do everything at home and the office "the places would fall apart." Are they wrong? I don't know, but are they powerless and unhappy? Absolutely. Do they think they are the main player in their lives? Not at all.

Occasionally, it's the circumstances that seem to be the focus of my clients' stories. Many women I come in contact with have stayed home for years to raise the kids. They now feel that the work world has changed, and they don't have the relevant skills to get a job. Other women I speak with blame their genes for their inability to lose weight. Others say that they don't have time to work out, and therefore they can't shed the pounds. No doubt many of these grievances are valid, but they are dead-end conversations, because the women are not at the centre of their stories.

The problem is never what the people are doing. The problem is always caused by a person or persons, a situation or a circumstance outside of their control.

When you hear any complaint, or when you complain yourself, it's usually about someone else or something else.

My boss isn't listening to me. He only promotes those he likes.

My kids aren't listening to me.

My staff doesn't listen to me either.

They have more money, so I can't compete.

The industry is corrupt, so what can someone like me do?

They don't know what they are doing, so I have to do it all.

My spouse doesn't care.

She flaunts herself in front of me just to make me feel inadequate.

She's a flirt. How is my husband supposed to react? It's her fault.

He has ruined my life.

They think they are always right.

He/she just doesn't understand.

They're idiots.

No matter what I do, they...

They, they, they, they, they.

The premise of all these complaints is the same: It's *their* fault. You have nothing to do with it. Someone else, not you, is doing things to make you less successful and happy and fulfilled than you should be. Someone else has the power, not you. Or maybe the power resides in circumstances— the way the industry is these days, or the expectations you have for a life-style. Either way, you are telling yourself you don't have the power. It's somewhere else.

Why do we turn to excuses? Why do we blame? If we are really honest with ourselves, chances are we could point out some way we are ben-efiting from these complaints. Does complaining that a friend is taking advantage of us make us feel superior? Does blaming the economy for our poor performance excuse us from working harder? Does believing that our kids won't listen to us get us off the hook from making unpopular rules or decisions for the family? And if we didn't have an excuse to fall on, what would we be left with? Complaints, excuses, and blame produce what I call the "righteous juice." It's the power you get from being right and making someone or something wrong for your situation.

Exercise: Are you hanging out in the complaints department?

Make a list of all your complaints. List how long you have had each one and rate it on a scale of 1 to 10 (1 being not a big deal and 10 being a huge problem). Then try to figure out what you are getting out of each complaint. What is the underlying benefit you are getting from having it? Does keeping this particular one help you move forward or does it make you angry or frustrated each time you think of it? How often do you say to yourself, "I don't care what they think, I'm right about this"? Are these complaints making you happy or keeping you from being happy? If they are keeping you from being happy, it's time to do something about them. You may perceive that having these complaints benefits you in some way, but it's not a positive benefit. What you get in return is disguised as a benefit, but in reality it is stealing your love, your happiness, your fulfillment.

The following chart shows an example to help you uncover your complaints, identify how long they have been around, and assess what you are ultimately getting from keeping this complaint around. If you weren't getting the juice of the complaint, you wouldn't have it.

Complaint	I hate my job	I'm overweight
How long	5 years	15 years
Rating	9	3
Who is to blame?	My boss	My schedule because I can't eat right or work out
What am I getting out of it?	I get to be right that he's a bully. I'm not going to work hard for someone like him.	I get to be right that I'm so busy and important that I just don't have time to work out. I can feel I have a right to look the way I do.

A blank form to use for your own complaints is found in the Appendix, on page 148.

In this example, you can see that the person who thinks her boss is a bully focuses on being right and on getting back at her boss by not putting effort into her work, which in turn causes her to hate her job—the initial complaint. Can you see the vicious circle that is created? Can you see the benefit she gets from having this complaint? She gets to be right. We all love to be right, and being right is disguised as a benefit but really it creates a wall between you and any happiness in the situation. The woman who blames her schedule for her lack of weight loss also insists she is right that she is just too busy to attend to her health. She too is creating a vicious circle of complaint and righteousness. The biggest juice people get from their complaints is being right about them, thereby avoiding responsibility for the result. And as you can see, the complaint doesn't go away. Until you can see what you are getting out of it, what the juice is, what the disguised benefit is, you will keep the complaint around. So the question is this: What's more important—being right and maintaining the grievance or doing something about it so you can be happy? How many wars are started because one side thinks it is right? All of them! Is being right helpful? Does it create happiness, love, or fulfillment? How open are you to others when you are being right?

From your chart, choose which complaint you want to rid yourself of first. See what the juice is that you're getting and how it is perpetuating this complaint. Then choose what is more important, the complaint or your happiness. In Chapter 3, "How to Get Your Power Back," you'll learn more about how to change your behaviour and your attitude so that you can move past these complaints.

Missing Power? You Gave It Up

Complaints aren't just about how you tell your stories or see your life. They aren't just about "pretending" that you aren't in control (like the teenager who blamed his crappy car for the accident). They often reflect how you are actually operating and the fact that you really have given over the power in your life.

Think back to your 20s. Chances are, anything seemed possible back then. Perhaps you were brimming with confidence. You didn't care if you had no experience or the job didn't pay well. Or maybe you were uncertain about where you wanted to live, who you wanted to be with, what kind of career would make you happy. So you started something, and if that wasn't working, you dropped it and took another path. You kept your eyes open for opportunities; you tried new things; you saw the possibilities. But whether you were certain about what you were doing or were searching for direction, you were the protagonist, the lead actor in that life.

Somewhere along the line, you gave up your power. You probably weren't conscious of it, but if you're in this position, living a 6 out of 10 life, you did.

Take Sally: Sally lives in a great apartment, a cosy place decorated in the warm colours of Provence. She loves it. Then she meets Peter. His apartment is straight contemporary—geometric shapes, black and white, odd-shaped couches that look like they belong in a design museum. When Sally moves in with Peter, they agree to sell everything and start over. Everything that goes into the apartment has to be approved by both of them. Not surprisingly, Peter vetoes 90% of the things Sally buys, and she vetoes 90% of what he likes. Eventually she gives up. Peter takes on the role of chief designer; the only things she buys for the home are towels, sheets, and kitchen gadgets. She likes the contemporary look, but it doesn't feel like her home. She has given up her power to him, and this is now their pattern. It started in decorating, then moved to their travel, and now it's in all areas of her life. Now it's just the way it is.

You can give up power in many parts of your life.

You can give up your power at work.

Take Anne: She's a teacher. She has no control over her salary and is constantly frustrated by the politics of her job. The actions of unions, politicians, parents, kids, the school board, as well as the principals and other teachers, affect her every day. She truly feels that she is at the mercy of all the moving parts of the education system and that she has no power of her own. And that demotivates her. After years of being a great teacher for her kids and her school, she feels that her efforts have made no difference, so she no longer puts so much of herself into her work. She is now just doing her job. She gets no joy, no sense of accomplishment, and no satisfaction from it. She has given up the power she once had—the power to change the lives of her students and to create enjoyment for herself.

Or you can give up your power to your husband and kids.

Take Molly: Molly has put her career on hold for eight years while raising her three children. Now she's a taxi driver, housekeeper, handyman, and short-order cook. At the end of each day, her husband thinks she just watched TV and ate lunch with friends. He wants her to go back to work and help bring in some money. She can't because of them—the kids, the husband, the employers who aren't likely to hire someone like her. Now she feels trapped.

And you can give up your power to a difficult circumstance.

Take Marie: Her husband has ended the marriage, and she is trying to manage living a whole new life. But if going through the divorce wasn't hard enough, the issues that come along with the split are frustrating and disheartening. She hates dealing with friends who now feel like they need to take sides, or an ex-husband who seems more interested in being single than being a father, or the married women who don't want a beautiful single woman in their midst. She is anxious about being financially dependent on her ex, and she is worried that her kids are blaming themselves and are suffering. She complains to friends who have taken her side, looking for sympathy and validation, but she doesn't seem to realize that she's given up the power that comes with taking charge of her life and her choices. She is so busy blaming her husband and the difficulties that come with divorce that she's given up working on her independence or happiness.

And you can give your power up to jealousy.

Take Melanie: Her husband had an affair. Okay, I bet you think you know where this is going. Melanie blamed her husband, right? Wrong. Melanie, like so many women, blamed the other woman. She saw her as a predator, a home wrecker, even though the affair had been mutual. And yet Melanie chose to see not only herself but also her husband as a victim, allowing her to create a "poor us" bond with him. She refused to take responsibility for her own part in the marriage dysfunction or to make her husband do the same. Where is the power here? If you blame the breakdown of your relationship on someone else outside the relationship, how do you have any power? You can't change anything, you can't learn any lessons, and you will most likely set yourself up for a repeat performance.

In fact, jealousy of other women because they are smart, beautiful, sexy, alluring, funny, and so many other things, is just showing the world what you think of yourself and allowing others to have far too great an impact on your happiness. It is just one more way of giving up your power.

All these stories illustrate the same point: When you lose power over your life, when you lose control over what you do, you lose some of the pleasure and joy and fulfillment of life itself. Happiness is based on freedom—the freedom to choose, the freedom to create your own life, and feel in control of your success and your failures. It's the freedom to learn, the freedom to find happiness and fulfillment in a way that suits you.

You know you've handed over your power to someone or something when

- You complain about something—again and again.
- You feel frustrated or angry at someone.
- Someone gives you advice, and you say "Yeah but"—or make an excuse for why you are right and someone or something is wrong.
- You doubt yourself in the face of someone else's opinions or thoughts.
- You blame someone or something for the way your life has turned out.
- You feel victimized by someone or some situation.
- You feel stuck or paralyzed.

Don't Sell Out on Yourself

If you give up your power over your life, if you abdicate control, you're losing more than you may realize.

You're selling out on yourself. You're saying that you don't matter. Other things or other people matter more than you do. This may sound selfless, almost laudable, but it's not. If you are doing this because you have lost the power to say or do what you want, you pay a massive penalty.

You will diminish your self-worth. That is a lot harder to handle than the loss of a Saturday night date or a job. If you do this, you make yourself small, and then, when things don't work out, you're not just getting over the loss of job or guy; you're getting over the loss of yourself. You gave up on you.

But there's an important proviso: You have to pick your battles and decide what really matters for you. If you don't care that much about cooking or about home design, then of course you can hand that task over to your spouse. Or perhaps you can see that for your spouse, it's really important to spend a week a year at the family cottage. You might say to yourself, *I will go there and enjoy it because I can see it's important to him.* That is a powerful choice to make. If, on the other hand, you're doing it only because you feel you have to, you'll be resentful and unhappy. You've given up power unwillingly, and that won't be good for you or anyone around you.

If this sounds familiar, you have plenty of company. We do this all the time, especially when we're resisting change or when we're afraid to see something end.

As an executive coach, I often see this syndrome at work. Take the former marketing vice-president who starts working for a high-level executive on a consulting basis. The executive treats the former VP like a personal assistant. He asks her to take notes and get coffee at the meetings, organize meetings, and make sure packages are delivered. She feels belittled, deflated, unimportant. But she doesn't say anything. Why? She's afraid of getting fired, losing her paycheque. She's lost control over her work life, and her happiness at work. She also loses so much more. She loses herself, her self-respect, in her own eyes and his as well.

I also see it in the personal lives of my clients. The woman whose husband has cheated on her does not leave even though she feels rejected by him and knows she will never trust him again. She sells out on herself because of fear or denial or guilt about her children. She may even try to turn things around by finding ways to get him to love her again. This attempt to get someone back is riddled with techniques of doing what you think the other person wants in order to change their point of view; however, to do this you will typically sell out on yourself and your needs, and lose your power in the process, leaving you feeling even more dejected.

You can see this unhappy story play out, again and again, at home and at work. You find yourself in a position that makes you unhappy, but you're afraid to do something because you might lose the spouse or the job and the money that goes with both. Sometimes you can't stand to think about the optics of making a change. You don't want to be seen as the one with the failed marriage, as the job quitter, or as the single parent.

In our society, we're supposed to think of other people first. This is rewarded and treasured, and rightly so. But if you do this and sell out on your own happiness and aspirations, how does that make you feel? Resentful? Regretful?

How will that affect your feelings about yourself? How will it affect the way you deal with your spouse, your co-workers and employees, and your own children? Don't you think that resentment will come out?

At this stage, I'm not advocating leaving (in the case of a marriage, for example) or changing anything (in the case of a job, perhaps)—I am just pointing out what might be going on. You don't have to think about doing anything quite yet because there are many other power tools to consider before taking such a large step.

Being Powerless: Being a Victim

If I asked you if you were a "victim," you probably would say no, unless you had recently suffered a serious injury from a crime or an accident. In fact, you may have immediately said, "Not me!" and felt offended or put off by the suggestion that you were any sort of victim. But after reading the previous pages, you might confess to feeling stuck, frustrated, unhappy, or dissatisfied. You might have also recognized that when you talk about the things that bother you, you aren't the main player in the story. Perhaps you've even admitted to yourself that you tend to make excuses or see other people or outside forces as the cause of at least some of your problems. And maybe you realize that you have given away some or all of your power.

If this is how you are behaving, I would argue that you are feeling like a victim. A victim, after all, is defined as someone who is harmed by another or by an action or event. In fact, these days we use the word "victim" to describe anyone who has had a setback that is not her fault. We may be "victims" of the recession, bad weather, or even chaos at the airport. So if you feel as if you are at the mercy of someone or something else, trapped by your circumstances, if you blame others for your problems or feel others have all the power, then you have essentially cast yourself as a victim.

Keep in mind, however, that most of us behave or feel like victims only now and then, or only when it comes to certain situations. But for women, there tend to be a number of areas in which we are likely to feel more powerless than men once in a while—whether it's working in a male-dominated industry, navigating the dating world, or juggling the demands of motherhood. (If, however, we adopt the role of "victim" in every aspect of our lives, if it becomes our identity, then we've fallen into the Victim Mindset Trap, which I will discuss in Chapter 4, "Beware of the Traps.")

The good news is that once you realize you are feeling or behaving like a victim, you can start to change all of that: You've taken the first step to getting your power back!

3

How to Get Your Power Back

You don't have to live feeling frustrated, unhappy, stuck, or like a victim. You can get back the personal power you once had. Or you can access the power you never had. You have the power to change your thoughts, your behaviours, your actions, and your reactions. You don't have to turn your life upside down; you can actually find the power to make your life better.

You can do it if you consider this possibility: It's not them or your circumstances; it's you. You can embrace what I call "The YOU Factor."

In other words, stop talking about them, stop talking about it, and start thinking about you. Begin this day on a simple premise: You are in charge of you! Only you. No one else.

For many people this is a big shift. It's a different mindset because they're so used to seeing themselves as a pawn in someone else's game. But if you recognize that you truly are in control of your life, you will find this new mindset so powerful it will change your world.

This can be especially hard for women to do because so many of us are driven by a deep need to connect and bond. This need influences the way we deal with our marriages, our children, our friends, and our jobs. We pour ourselves into our relationships and do all kinds of things to make our personal connections function. When we marry, have aging parents, and are responsible for children, we dial down our own ambitions and personal desires to make our loved ones' lives more happy and secure. Because we're driven by a deep need to bond, it's easy to overlook what we want, what we need. Yet if we do this, we may not realize that we can end up in a life where we're taking care of everyone except ourselves.

Just knowing you have a choice will give you a new feeling of freedom. It will free you, even if you choose to keep doing what you are doing. You can say to yourself, *Okay, I have made a choice to scale back on my career while my kids are young because I want to be at home when they come back from school, but I can always make a different choice later.* Or: *I have chosen to stay in this job, even though I don't like it, because it pays for a house and a lifestyle that I love. I can always change that decision at a later date.*

The Big Truth: Believe It or Not, You Got Yourself Into This

This may come as a surprise: You are where you are today because of choices you made. In other words, you got yourself into this.

This sounds crazy, right?

You might be saying to yourself: *It's not my fault that I'm underpaid, even though the work I do is really hard.* Well, who chose that job? Who chose to keep it?

You might be saying: *It's not my fault that my marriage is a bit dull. My spouse doesn't talk to me any more, and we don't do anything together. It's not like the old days....* Well, who chose that spouse? And more important, what about you? Are you contributing to the marriage in the way you once did?

Here's the hardest one: *It's not my fault that I got sick.* No, of course it is not. But, as we are about to see, you are making a choice about how you handle your illness today, right at this moment.

Here's an example. One of my clients, a vice-president of finance, came to me one day with a common complaint. She had no time to do her work: "Everyone comes to me with their problems, and I'm the one who has to solve them. I'm the only one who has the information."

She was working for a large company, and every day employees three levels down from her would file into her office with minor problems, like what to do with the contractor who didn't get a quote in on time, or how to resolve a routine conflict. They should have figured it out themselves, or asked their boss rather than the VP. But she let them in. She listened to their problems, and solved them efficiently. She actually created the situation by always saying yes. That created a problem for her: She was so busy solving everyone else's little dilemmas that she didn't have time to deal with the big ones on her desk. It looked to her like it was everyone else causing her stress and time issues, but soon she could see it was actually her.

This does not mean you should launch into the it's-all-my-fault mode either. Blaming yourself doesn't help. However, if you take responsibility for the choices you have made up to now, and recognize you made choices that put yourself in the situation where you are now, you have taken the first step to regaining power over your life. After all, if you got yourself into this, you can get yourself out.

1
POWER TOOL

Power Tool 1: Accept Responsibility

Look at all the stories I told in Chapter 2, "Where Did My Power Go?" In almost every case, part of giving up power was refusing to take responsibility for your choices or for making changes. Clearly, the teen with the car was all about shirking his responsibility! But the women were also refusing to take ownership of their problems and their lives. Anne wasn't happy teaching any more, but she hadn't taken responsibility for finding ways she could work happily within the system or for considering career moves that might provide her with an enjoyable work environment. Molly was frustrated by the demands of her family, but she had taken no responsibility for the fact that she had set up the domestic routine the way she did. And while she felt that her work-related skills had atrophied, she wasn't taking responsibility for re-educating herself. And Marie, consumed with bitterness and hurt, simply wasn't taking responsibility for the fact that she was living in the past instead of moving forward.

But what of Melanie? Her husband had an affair. Should she really have to take responsibility for that? As I implied in Melanie's story, she does have to take responsibility for some of what unfolded. She might be responsible in part for a marriage that had grown stale or dysfunctional. But even if she was working her hardest at the relationship, perhaps she had married a man who simply was a philanderer, or maybe she was out of touch with his needs, or possibly they were just growing apart and living separate lives. There are so many reasons why affairs occur. However, the fact is that this situation is now a part of her life and she needs to deal with it powerfully. Typically, women blame the other woman; if she had not preyed on the husband, he would never have strayed. She's not holding him responsible, then. That is the problem, because they both become victims of the other woman. This leaves all the power in the other woman's hands. This doesn't help. Melanie has to hold her husband responsible for his actions, and she has to take responsibility for herself so that she can make powerful choices.

Sometimes it may seem unfair because you didn't create the situation you are in, but taking responsibility for your life is an absolutely necessary step in getting your power back.

What does it mean to take responsibility for your life? Taking responsibility means employing "The YOU Factor." It means realizing that you are the writer, the main actor, the director, and the producer of your story. Although there will be people and circumstances that affect your life, you and only you are in charge of your happiness. Do you find yourself saying:

He doesn't ...

She doesn't ...

I wish ...

They never ...

They always ...

I'm always the one ...

Why can't ...

Why me ...

Every time you catch yourself complaining, or saying "they," ask yourself: What can I do about it right now? When you think over what happened in the past, ask yourself what role you played in the situation. Did you choose to be in that poisonous corporate climate? If your relationship unravelled, did you have anything to do with it? By exploring these questions, you may find you were an active player. You made that choice, so you have power and control over your life. If you do not believe that's the case, consider this: You cannot change the past. Neither anger, resentment, remorse, nor regret will alter one thing—in fact these emotions are causing you to hold on to it. Think of all the areas in your life where you feel you are not in control. Then look at who or what is the cause of your complaint or unhappiness, and then look at the ways you can regain power by taking responsibility for your issue. Once you begin to examine all the people and circumstances you are blaming for your unhappiness, you will notice one thing: Who the common denominator is in these complaints. Look in the mirror and honestly ask yourself who is at the core of all of these complaints ... YOU.

The intention of this exercise is to show how you can see the areas where you are not accepting responsibility in your life. Here is an example of what I mean.

Areas in my life where I am stuck or unhappy	Wanted to return to work after years of staying home with the family leaves me feeling unhappy and stuck.
Who or what is the cause of my unhappiness or complaint?	1. The kids and my husband, to whom I dedicated myself to raise the family. 2. The business world, which doesn't perceive raising a family as a transferable skill. 3. Regretting the choice of staying home that I made at the time.
In what ways can I take responsibility?	I take responsibility for making the choice to stay home and raise my children and give up my career. No one else is to blame for that.

A blank form to use for **Power Tool 1: Accept Responsibility** is found in the Appendix, on page 149.

What you can control is that you are responsible for everything you have in your life right now, how you perceive your world, and what you do about it.

Choose the Way You React

To regain power over your life, start with this: You always have a choice. Always. You cannot change what has already happened, of course, but you can always choose how you will react right now. And the beauty is that no one can stop you from deciding how you will react—even if what happened was out of your control!

To do this, you have to make an important distinction—between what happened and the meaning you give to the event that happened. It's easy to confuse the two. Many of us fuse them, so we think that if something happens, our reaction is a logical consequence of that event. We might even assume it's the only possible response to that event. This really limits our leeway to act.

Say you just missed a promotion or you lost a competition. There's one thing you cannot change—the event itself. However, you are in control of the meaning you give to that event and your reaction.

Or take a more personal example. A few years ago, I met Penny. She had given birth to a boy with Down's syndrome. She was angry with the world. She asked and asked "Why me?" She didn't want to bond with her son or even admit he was hers for the first few weeks of his life. It took everything in her to finally put aside her judgments, her fears of the future, her sadness for her little boy, and so many other emotions I will never know or understand so that she could just be his mother. After a few weeks, she realized there was nothing the anger, disappointment, or sense of unfairness could change. She had a son, she was his mother, and she needed to be the best one she could. She could not change her circumstances. What happened, happened. All she could do was change how she was looking at her situation. It didn't take long before all her negative emotions became positive. Now she can see the blessing this little boy is and be grateful for the joy he has brought to her family. He has changed her life in ways she would have never imagined.

Accepting responsibility means looking at your role in everything that happens or has happened in your life. Even though there will be situations in your life that appear to be beyond your control, you still need to look in the mirror and take responsibility for how you will respond to them.

A client asked his broker many years ago to sell a stock when the price was at a point where my client would have come out ahead. She encouraged him to hold on, thinking the price would still go up. It plummeted two days later. Within two days, my client had gone from the possibility of making money to losing 75% of his investment. He knew he couldn't change what had happened, and as much as he would have loved to yell and scream at his broker for leading him astray, telling her how incompetent she was, he didn't. Instead he took responsibility for not listening to his own instincts and not demanding she execute the sell. He also took responsibility for investing in the first place. He realized that if he wasn't comfortable losing the investment, he shouldn't have played the market. He now handles his investments very differently. He learned a hard lesson but is aware that this was all his own doing.

It's about how we react.

Our brain's first response is to go into the fight-or-flight mode. This may cause to you to be vindictive and vengeful, angry and irate, or even depressed and withdrawn. Your reactions can drive you into the pit of anger and resentment. As the anger takes over, it influences the way you behave right now. And when you're angry, or vindictive, or even sad, it's hard to consider all the options, see other perspectives, and make the best possible choice under the circumstances. In this state of heightened emotion, you have no power.

But even if you can't control the circumstances, you can always control how you react. This may not be easy or happen immediately; however, knowing that there is another way to see your situation, that you can find a way out of the powerlessness, will provide you with a sense that there is a light at the end of this proverbial tunnel.

Choose How You Think and Feel

Part of taking full responsibility is choosing your thoughts and feelings. Yes, this may sound odd. You may be saying, "But you can't stop the way you think or feel. If I feel it, it must be valid, and if I think it, it must be true." Well, that isn't necessarily true. The fact is you can choose your feelings. You also can choose your thoughts. You may have feelings arrive uninvited, but you can dismiss the ones you don't want and replace them with others. Let me explain.

A client was having a very tough time in her marriage. She and her husband fought a lot. As soon as he came home from the office, she would be on guard. Even before he arrived, she would get anxious and angry about his complaints. Then one day, she decided to adopt a different emotion. She chose to be calm and to be happy that he was home. Instead of getting anxious, she would calm herself down and decide to be more relaxed and easygoing. When her husband arrived home, she smiled and gave him a kiss; she told him she was glad he was home. Her new way of behaving caused him to relax too. Her change in attitude even spilled over into her behaviour with her kids. From then on, the evenings were very different.

Now as far as thoughts go, you may not be able to choose what pops into your head, but you can choose what thoughts you act upon. For example, your child is late coming home from school. You wonder if something has happened to her, and then you start to panic. We can all imagine the range of thoughts and emotions that are then put into play. But just because you thought for a split second that something might have happened to your child, you do not have to believe that or act upon it. You can choose a different thought, like, *Hmm, she's later than usual, but I'm sure she's fine. I'll give her a call in five minutes if she's not home.* Or you might wonder whether she told you she had plans after school and you have forgotten.

Here's another example: Your direct report misses an important deadline. You are furious. This reflects poorly on you and the department, not to mention putting all the other project deadlines at risk. You can't change what happened now. The report is not done and no matter how angry you get, it will not get the report completed.

Being able to consciously choose your thoughts and feelings will keep you empowered and peaceful. It will even provide a sense of control.

Your Stories

Life is about stories. The stories we tell each other. The stories we tell ourselves. Our stories define who we are.

Our stories start to be written as soon as we experience life. Stories can strengthen us, make us successful and happy and fulfilled. Or they can weaken us, undermine our drive, poison our hopes. We might start out life with a story that inspires us to great success at work and to a life in a world full of love and connection, but then, as our lives change and get more complicated, that story might not play any more. It can turn against us, and we don't even know it.

Take a page, or 10, and write your story. Write your entire story, all of it. Just the way you remember it. Read it to yourself a couple of times. What do you think? Is it true?

Is Your Story True?

As we grow up, events in our lives propel us to create stories about the world and our relationship to it. For example, if, as a child, we told our parents small lies and consistently got away with that, we might create a narrative that tells us that minor deceptions are useful. We have crafted a story about ourselves, about others, and about life in general based on our past actions and decisions. As we move forward, this story will determine other actions and decisions we make. And we will insert the events of our day into that story and make judgments accordingly, perhaps developing other narratives as we go. We will use the stories we have developed to determine what or who is right, wrong, good, or bad.

This is not a process, however, that we are necessarily aware of. Our stories lie deep inside us, so deep, in fact, that we often don't realize that they are having an effect on us or that they can be changed. And this can be a problem.

The problem with our stories is that they are based on the past, not the present. Think about the lying example. The story was created when you were a small child, but your adult life is probably still being guided by the same narrative. Maybe the story you've told yourself about the harmlessness of lies has led to dishonesty in your marriage—or on your tax forms. Maybe it's actually creating problems for you now with your spouse or with the Canada Revenue Agency.

Many of our stories are more complicated or nuanced than this example, but they can imprison us, leading to decisions that are no longer effective. Rather than helping explain our world, they can be holding us back.

But even our "new" stories can lead us astray. We often take a few bits of information, gleaned from friends, a newspaper, hearsay, or what we think we saw or heard, and create a narrative. Then we tell it to ourselves as if it were the truth. It may or may not correspond to the truth, but it's our narrative, our reality, and most importantly, it affects the way we feel and what we do as a result. But what if this story has a negative impact on our happiness or propels us in the wrong direction? If we are struggling in some area of our life, we need to put the stories we tell ourselves under the microscope, question their validity, and ask ourselves, *Are they true?*

Let's take a simple example. You send an email to a colleague requesting something, and he doesn't respond. You start telling yourself all kinds of stories. He's an inconsiderate idiot. He doesn't think I'm important enough. He thinks I'm an idiot. He thinks my work is really bad.

Think of how that affects you right away. If those thoughts run through your mind, how do you feel? How does that affect the way you deal with that person when you see him? What impact will that have on you?

This is a simple example but it illustrates the same story that plays out in many aspects of our lives.

Something happens. We turn that into a story, embellished with plenty of emotions and "facts" that we have created.

We react to our narrative—not to what actually happened.

Let's go back to the email example. What do you know for sure? You know you sent an email, and your colleague didn't respond. The rest is your own conjecture. You made it up. The fact is, you don't know why your colleague didn't answer.

The first antidote to the story trap is to get rigorous on the reality check.

Check out the facts. Email or call your colleague and say, "I was concerned I hadn't heard from you."

Take responsibility by saying, "I sent an email, and I'm not sure it got through." Don't blame your colleague by asking why he didn't respond.

Maybe your email was caught in a spam filter. Maybe your colleague was so busy that he forgot to reply to your message. Maybe the reason had nothing to do with what you thought.

To gain power over your life, you need to separate fact from fiction.

If you got passed over for a job, you might say, "The boss chose George because they're golfing buddies." But that is not the fact. You are assuming that George got the job because he has a single-digit handicap, and he's a good guy. The only fact you know for sure is that George got the job—not you. There might be all kinds of reasons why George got the job. Maybe this job required a high level of interpersonal skills and George has it—just look at him work a room at a conference or a party. Maybe it's something else. The fact is, you don't know.

Here's another example. You weren't invited to a party, and it seems that everyone else in your circle was. You might tell yourself that the host doesn't like you or that you did something to offend her. Or you might think that she was just being mean. These thoughts will make you fume. You will no doubt feel left out and miserable.

How's that working for you?

The fact is, you don't know why you were not on the party list. Everything you've told yourself is a story, not the fact.

Women tend to internalize more than men and so are apt to put themselves in a negative light when interpreting situations. (How often have you thought someone was giving you a funny look and decided that she didn't like you or you must have just said something stupid?) For that reason, it's especially important for women to find out as much information as possible, so we don't ruminate negatively. And if we don't know what others are thinking and are going to make up a story, why not make it positive? Make up something that will make you feel good about yourself instead of bad. Make your story empowering. So instead of saying, "She clearly doesn't like me, that's why she didn't want me at her party," you might say, "She must not know how to approach me; maybe she's a little shy or intimidated."

Or if you weren't asked on a sales pitch, and you can't find out why, perhaps your story could be that you are such a great boss they knew the juniors would be able to handle it, and you weren't needed on this one.

None of this is to say you lie to yourself or live with rose-coloured glasses on. It's just a different way to look at the situation. It will show you both sides. And since both are made up by you, you may as well err on the happy side.

Once you realize what is and isn't real, you automatically gain power. You are no longer making decisions on the basis of a negative story that may not be true. You don't waste time complaining that your neighbour or your boss is treating you badly. You do not create a black cloud of resentment that can turn anyone off, including your friends. By separating fact from fiction, you can change the way you perceive the picture.

As you move forward in your life, you need to look at your stories carefully. If you can identify the part of your story that is not true or that may reflect your past rather than your present, you can take it off your list. It will cease to have power over you.

2
POWER TOOL

Power Tool 2: Check Your Story

What actually happened? What do I know for sure?

Events that happen in our lives are shared as stories. The stories you tell yourself about what happens in your life come from your beliefs, your past experiences, and your assumptions, and these in turn give way to your behaviours, your actions and reactions. When something happens, you tell yourself a story, embedded with the drama and emotion of the moment.

The power in this power tool is to be aware of what's fuelling your stories and questioning what part is fact and what part is just the "stuff" you've layered onto it.

Here is an example that distinguishes between the story and the facts.

What's my story?	My boss promoted my co-worker because she is single and childless.
What is my story stripped down to just the facts?	I didn't get the promotion.
What did I add to the facts?	Someone else got the promotion because she has more time and therefore looks more committed.

A blank form to use for **Power Tool 2: Check Your Story** is found in the Appendix, on page 149.

Take an event that has happened to you; it could be from the past week or the story of your life, which you wrote earlier.

Look carefully at your story, what happened, the facts, and what you have layered onto it.

Where Else Do Your Stories Come From?

You've heard people say "Everyone has a story to tell." And that's true. Of course, some stories are more compelling than others, and some are greatly embroidered to make them into a dramatic narrative. What kind of storyteller are you?

3
POWER TOOL

Power Tool 3: Looking at Your Belief System and Personal Truths

If you have discovered that you are telling yourself stories that are not true or not helpful, you may find yourself wondering about some of the other ways you created these little narratives and how you can guard against creating other inaccurate or misleading stories in the future. In order to break away from storytelling that constrains us rather than frees us, we have to look at where these stories come from. As much as our narratives are created by our past, they are also based on our belief system. Our belief system comes from our upbringing and what we are taught and told by our parents, teachers, peers, society, etc. We may feel strongly about the importance of community or of individual freedom, for example. We may have been brought up to believe honesty is the best policy or we may feel that kindness outweighs all else. We are usually fairly conscious of these kinds of thoughts and how they inform our stories. But there are other areas that we may not be so aware of: personal truths, belief systems, assumptions, and perspective.

Now let me be honest. I use the word "truths" but very often what I am describing is the exact opposite. "Personal truths" is the way I describe all those individual assertions that we believe to be true. These ideas are what drive us; they help us fashion our stories; they inform all our decisions and our attitudes. These are beliefs that we rarely if ever question. Sometimes we aren't even aware that we hold them.

Some of our "truths" might be quite empowering (and may in fact be "true"). For example:

I'm a good person: My instincts are sound, and I usually treat others fairly.

Hard work will bring results: I can overcome difficulties and produce good work by putting in a little extra elbow grease.

The world doesn't revolve around me: It's important for me to see the big picture and take the views of others into account.

I love to learn: I learn from every experience, and the learning indicates that I am moving toward where I want to be.

People are trustworthy: I just have to trust first. If I trust first, instead of waiting for people to prove themselves, I find that people are more reliable than many may think.

Life is fun, a wonderful challenge: Who ever said life was easy or fair? When a problem comes up, it's a challenge, a puzzle to be solved. Every obstacle is a step toward helping me grow and be successful.

But others can be far less helpful. In fact, they may be overly critical, disempowering, or harmful.

I'm not cut out for success: It takes too much responsibility, time, and effort to be successful. Besides, rich people are snobs, or corrupt. Successful people aren't happy. They don't have time for anything other than work.

I can't afford to take risks: What if I try and fail? What does that say about me? What will people think or say?

No one likes me: I don't belong. I don't join in with the group because I know I won't be accepted.

I'm not good enough: I need one more degree to do what I want. I need to read one more book before I submit that article. I need to practise more before I shoot for the top.

I'm not loveable: Maybe if I pretend to be somebody else, I will be loved.

Life is a struggle: Life is hard. You can't win.

People are mean, dishonest, or selfish: If they get a chance, they will cheat and lie.

These beliefs or "personal truths" that we tell ourselves govern what we notice, what we take in, and how we view it. This in turn affects the way we behave. An empowering personal truth will push us toward reaching our goals, being happier, and enjoying life, feeling in control of our life's path. A limiting personal truth holds us back and even distracts us from our goals and our enjoyment of life; it robs us of our power, our feeling of control, and our happiness.

Our personal truths and the stories they lead to are so powerful they can guide our lives without our even knowing it. What if one of your personal truths is that you aren't worthy of love? What kind of mate do you think you might choose? What kind of compromises might you make in order to have any kind of love in your life? Or what if you thought rich people were snobs or crooks? How much money do you think you'd be making? How successful would you be in business if your story was that you had to give up your time and your happiness in order to be successful? Can you see how our truths and our stories really create and mould our current reality? And yet we have made it all up. Who said any of it is true? Only you do.

Disempowering "Truths"

I am a failure.

Life is hard and full of problems.

I'm too afraid.

Everyone is against me.

I have no choice.

It's not my fault.

Denial is a solution.

I'm a weak person.

People are judgmental.

Empowering "Truths"

I am trying and learning.

Life is full of challenges.

I'm nervous or excited.

People are essentially good.

I always have a choice.

I'm responsible for my actions.

Denying it does not make it
go away.

I'm a capable person.

I'm likeable.

Exercise: Uncovering your beliefs and personal truths.

How do you find out what some of those truths and beliefs are that are affecting your life? When you recall frustrating situations that left you feeling bad about yourself and continue to make you feel that way, you are likely holding on to a personal truth. Personal truths are hidden; you don't see them, and they are tough to identify.

This example demonstrates a way to uncover our personal truths and see how they affect us.

A recurring situation that makes me react in a particular way	I fight with my husband about his ex-wife and I'm left feeling second best.
What is my personal truth?	I'm not worthy of love or I'm not lovable.
What effect does my belief in that personal truth have on my life?	I never really feel completely loved by others.
What is the opposite truth?	I am lovable and worthy.
How would my situation change if I held that opposite truth?	I would see that he is with me and loves me. His issues with her are separate from me.
Should I change it?	Yes/no

A blank form to use for **Power Tool 3: Look at Your Belief System and Personal Truths** is found in the Appendix, on page 150.

Once you have identified the personal truths that are controlling you, you may need to change the ones that are leading to misunderstandings or resentments and adjust those that aren't useful.

Assumptions

Assumptions are beliefs and personal truths that we are not conscious of, that we take entirely for granted. And usually when I use the word "assumption" in my work, I use it to refer to those hidden beliefs that reflect how we think the external world operates. Some very specific examples might be our assumptions that our technology will work when we go to use it, that our car will start or the subway will arrive. We have assumptions about the stability of our world: the office building we work in will be there in the morning, our job will be there the next day, or our spouse will continue to be our spouse. Sometimes our assumptions reflect common experience (the way things unfold for most of the population): we assume we will recover from a cold or that our kids will outlive us.

Our assumptions about life and people and how the world works start to form from an early age. They're useful for everyday life: If you assume the bus will take you to work, you can use your mental space to be more productive in other areas. Think how shocked you are as a parent when the school calls to tell you your child hit another child. We assume our child will not behave like that. However, like our personal truths, these assumptions soon become "the way it is." A fact.

Yet assumptions aren't facts. And because of this, often they aren't really as useful as they seem, and they can even stop being helpful. For example, many parents think that strangers are a danger for kids. But that's an assumption. We have been led to feel this way, yet children are rarely abducted or molested by strangers; the perpetrators are frequently people they know. Overemphasizing the danger of strangers, therefore, is likely to frighten children unnecessarily without teaching them adequate self-protection.

Sometimes you maintain your assumptions because they reflect the way you would like to live. But as the old saying goes, wishing doesn't make it so. Studies have shown that we tend to attribute positive character traits to good-looking people. We might be hardwired to do this, but nevertheless it is an assumption. Expecting that the good-looking guy is going to be the man of your dreams may be what you would like to believe, but it's important to guard against an assumption like this. Good-looking guys can be scam artists, abusers, and cheaters too.

One of the most commonly held assumptions is this: We assume we understand what someone is trying to say, and we assume they understand what we're trying to say. In other words, we assume that other people understand us. Or put another way, we believe we speak the same "language." So, for example, your spouse says he wants to go away on a family trip. You say it's not a good idea right now. He had assumed you would be as excited as him about the idea and grateful for the suggestion. Now he assumes you don't want to go and are not appreciative of his outreach to spend time with you and the kids. You are, in fact, grateful. You really just meant the timing was bad because the kids were in exams and your work is very busy.

These assumptions are critical, because in communicating with others or dealing with people in business or personal relationships, we aim to hear and understand what people say. We hope they'll understand us too. What we fail to recognize is that we all bring a set of assumptions to the table, and when those assumptions are different, they can cause us to prematurely judge the other person or the situation.

Assumptions can affect our perception of simple things. As women, part of what makes us tick is connecting with others. Many women have a fundamental need to bond, so we like to have big "talks" with our husbands. Then, just as we're settling down on the couch with a glass of wine, they turn on the TV. We're unhappy. Then we blame our husband for not pulling his weight in the marriage. Yet take a look at our assumption. We're assuming they have the same need to bond that we do. They might not. For many men, the need to accomplish is a more powerful driver than the need to bond. So maybe they don't feel like having that deep talk. That's the way they are—for them, however, turning on the TV does not mean they're rejecting us. They just want to watch the ball game. That hunter/gatherer wiring takes men and women down very different paths and results in misunderstanding about what drives us, what we need, and how we act and react in situations. Learning about these gender differences can debunk many of our assumptions and lead us to a greater understanding of the opposite sex.

Assumptions also cause havoc in the dating world. Many women feel that a man should call the day after a date. If he doesn't, he's just not interested. Yet that's just an assumption—a rule that we made up. You might say it's a good one, but is that what the man assumes? Perhaps not. One of my clients had a more complicated set of assumptions when it came to dating. She had dated many men who she saw as not free with their feelings or played games by withholding their emotions. So when she met a new man who seemed to be different, she was leery. When their first relationship breakdown happened, she made all sorts of assumptions based on her past dating experiences. She assumed that if she raised the problem with him, he would tell her she was being too emotional, too sensitive, moving too quickly, or over-reacting. She was sure he would then walk away. It wasn't easy, but she decided to change her assumption and adopt a new empowering one that said every man was different. She reached out to her new man without her negative assumptions and had a very open and honest conversation with him. It is working out for them so far.

Our romantic lives, whether we're dating or married, are often a minefield of assumptions. This is largely because we start off with the whopper of them all—we assume that someone we feel attracted to will be our perfect match, possessing similar values, qualities, and characteristics as we do. If, for example, you are both active, love museums, and enjoy talking about philosophy, you might assume that that makes you great life partners. When it turns out you have very different views on money and religion, you ignore it. The earlier assumptions about how perfect you are as a couple keep you together and help you avoid dealing with your differences. But the assumption that the differences don't matter or will work themselves out, or even change over time, is where the relationship breakdowns happen.

We also assume that those we love can see when we are upset or hurt and then will do something to make us feel better. When this doesn't happen we are hurt and assume they must not love us as much as we thought. But just because someone cares for us doesn't mean that he or she can read our minds.

Look at what all these faulty assumptions do to you: They make you feel resentful, frustrated, and unhappy—about what you think those around you said or did, or did not do. So what's happened? You've just given up your power over your own happiness to that bristling feeling of resentment—a resentment that sprang from assumptions that may not have been valid or at least not shared.

And remember, if your assumptions about other people are creating problems, there's an easy fix. Just ask the person a direct question, something like:

What did you mean when you said that?
What is your understanding of my role in this organization?
Why did you act in that way?

These kinds of questions are useful in all your personal and business interactions. They help avoid potentially dangerous assumptions and they open up communication.

Any time an assumption is creating anger, resentment, frustration, vindictiveness, withdrawal, or any other negative emotion, you need to test it to see if it is valid. And you need to ask if the other person holds the same assumption.

In fact, if you want to create empowered and successful interactions, you have to uncover the assumptions you make about yourself, about others, and about the world in general. And then you have to adjust your attitudes and behaviour so that you can move forward in a positive way.

4
POWER TOOL

Power Tool 4: Challenge Your Assumptions

An assumption is something you accept as true without question or proof. It's something you take for granted. First, try to discover what assumptions you hold. You can look at the simple actions, habits, and attitudes in your life and see what assumptions are driving them.

Try to think about what has surprised, confounded, or baffled you in the past about the choices people have made, the ways they have lived their lives, their habits or customs, their parenting, or their ways of doing their jobs. You might also think about what has surprised you about your own life. What exactly has surprised you? In what ways did certain events go very differently from the way you thought they should or do work?

A few examples:

What surprised you: Your neighbour allows her nine-year-old to use the stove to make himself lunch.

The assumption that caused the surprise: It's unsafe to let anyone younger than a teen use the oven or stove.

What surprised you: Your sister does all the driving when she travels with her husband.

The assumption that caused the surprise: Men are better drivers than women.

Another assumption: Men always prefer to be the drivers.

What surprised you: The high school sweethearts who got married right after Grade 12 are still happily married.

The assumption that caused the surprise: Young love doesn't last.

What surprised you: Your nephew, who had a serious drug problem as a teenager, just graduated from law school.

The assumption that caused the surprise: If someone develops a drug habit, they can never get their life back on track.

What surprised you: You lost a bundle on your last house.

The assumption that caused the surprise: Real estate is always a safe investment.

Now that you have a list of assumptions, take a long hard look at them. Is there truth in any of them? How are they affecting your life? You may feel that some of your assumptions are still valid. Although your neighbour's son hasn't burned himself or set fire to the kitchen, you may still feel it is unwise to let your children use the stove until they are 11 or 12. But maybe you shouldn't be so dismissive of your teenage son's relationship with his girlfriend. And maybe next time you and your husband head off on a road trip, you should ask him if he wants to do the driving. Maybe there are other assumptions you should dismiss and make your judgments and decisions on a case-by-case basis.

Let's look at how our exercise from Power Tool 2: Check Your Story plays through when assumptions are added. As you add assumptions to your story, that story takes on different meaning yet again outside the basic facts.

What's my story?	My boss promoted my co-worker because she is single and childless.
What is my story stripped down to just the facts?	I didn't get the promotion.
What did I add to the facts?	That someone else got the promotion because she has more time and therefore looks more committed.
What are my assumptions about my story?	I assumed that she got the job only because my boss is concerned with an employee's ability to work around the clock.
What meaning have I given to my story based on those assumptions?	I made it mean that I got passed over because I'm a mother and my co-worker got the promotion for reasons other than her abilities.

A blank form to use for **Power Tool 4: Challenge Your Assumptions** is found in the Appendix, on page 151.

What are some of your assumptions and how do they affect your story?

Every time you find yourself surprised or even self-righteous about a situation or a person, ask yourself if you are working from an assumption. If so, examine if it is a valid assumption to hold on to.

Perspective

Your personal truths and assumptions often fashion the stories you create to explain the world, and there is another factor that influences those narratives: perspective. Imagine you're a photographer and you're shooting a picture of children running through the woods. Will you use a zoom lens and focus in on the children and the joy on their faces, or will you use a wide-angle lens to capture a mangy dog, an overflowing garbage can, and a large man in an overcoat prowling around in the background? The choice of your lens will alter your perception of the scene.

We all use a viewfinder to see our world, the people in it, and ourselves. We use this lens to navigate through life, just as a photographer chooses a lens to create a photograph. Yet unlike the photographer, most of us don't realize that we're using a lens to select and process the details we see in front of us. But this lens is crucial.

It affects what we see and what we recall. It influences everything we do or think.

Let's take something simple like paying the bills. For some people, paying bills causes great anxiety. When you pay your bills through the perspective that money is scarce, it causes you to relate to every dime that goes out as "I won't have anything left to pay for something else." What if you paid your bills with a different point of view? If you approached the task with the perspective that with every bill you paid your financial world was a little more secure, you might find yourself reassured instead of anxious. In other words, rather than looking at bill paying through the eyes of someone who is short of money, look at it through the eyes of someone who is in control of their finances.

Here's an example from another client on the value of looking at situations from another perspective. Every Christmas, he and his brothers would gather at their parents' home for a lovely dinner celebration. And every year, the goodbyes would go like this. He and his brothers would put on their coats, but not do them up since they were just going out to a heated running car. Their father would turn to the three of them and say, "Do up your coats, you'll catch your death of cold." My client's oldest brother would roll his eyes, shake his head, and walk away. The other brother would say, "I'm over 40 and can determine if I need my coat done up or not." My client, on the other hand, would give his dad a big hug. "Thanks for loving me, Dad." He looked at the situation through a different lens. Perhaps this was just his dad's way of telling them he cared and that he loved them. Perhaps he wasn't trying to treat them like little children. Unlike his brothers, though, my client found those goodbyes were moments of happiness, instead of frustration.

Despite the emergence of "positive" psychology, a vast majority of human beings look at the world from a negative perspective. A client, Sophia, has an inner critic, a voice that is always carping from the sidelines. She and I worked to identify the voice that reinforced the key decisions she had made in her youth. She came to realize that too frequently, her voice had a paralyzing effect. She didn't want to look at life through this perspective any more—she didn't want that voice to dictate how she perceived people, or situations, or her ensuing reaction. So we gave her inner critic a name—Dobby (from the Harry Potter books. This character also provided the visual of a creepy gremlin). At first, Sophia tried to ignore him, and she realized he then just screamed louder for attention. Sound crazy? Not at all. She now has conversations with Dobby when he turns up to voice his negative opinions. This is a way of separating that voice from her own thoughts and ideas. By talking to Dobby, she can keep him outside herself as a separate voice. She now also thanks him for trying to protect her or voice an opinion that may in fact be helpful. She acknowledges what he said and can objectively analyze his comments as something to seriously consider. These comments can then be added to the list of perspectives that she will look at when she makes her choices. This way, Dobby's point of view doesn't dominate and take over, and Sophia keeps her ability to see situations through a number of different lenses.

We do tend to see the world from our own vantage point. This limited perspective, along with our personal truths and assumptions, drives the stories we tell about ourselves and our situation. But we can challenge our personal truths and assumptions and get rid of belief systems that are no longer working for us by looking inward. And we can broaden our point of view, giving ourselves new understanding, options, and choice, by looking outward and seeing the world through the eyes of others.

5
POWER TOOL

Power Tool 5: View It From a Different Perspective

When we're stuck, we see only one solution, and we're sure we're right. At a time like this, we need to investigate all our options. A good way to do this is to look at our situation from different points of view. Seeing other people's perspectives is an important tool.

Here's one trick:

Ask yourself: What would Oprah do? What would Warren Buffett do? What would your mother do, your best friend, your boss, your spouse, or anyone else you respect?

Here's a way to view your problem from a different perspective—by using a visual aid!

I got passed over for a promotion.				
ME	**MENTOR**	**BOSS**	**MOTHER**	**OPRAH**
I have kids and can't commit to the time needed.	You don't have the full set of qualifications necessary to fill this position.	She got promoted because she is very good at her job.	It doesn't matter because you really can't commit the time needed for the new position.	Everything happens for the right reasons. It may be a blessing.

A blank form to use for **Power Tool 5: View It from a Different Perspective** is found in the Appendix, on page 152.

In the single rectangle in the middle, write your issue or problem. I have used the example above to give you an idea of how those perspectives came to be. Above each small rectangle, write the name of the individual whose opinions you respect. Be sure to include your name too.

Inside each rectangle, write what you think that person's perspective would be. Now look at all the different perspectives you have written down.

Be very open to the other perspectives and honest with your own. You may be emotionally attached to your perspective, yet that doesn't mean it's the right one. So you can elect to keep that perspective or one of the others on your diagram.

Take another look at your perspective. Did it influence the way you told your story in Power Tool 2? Would you tell a different story if you adopted a different perspective?

Adjust Your Personal Truth and Change Your Story

You have now looked at your stories, pulling fact from fiction by assessing your beliefs and personal truths, challenging your assumptions, and viewing different perspectives. In many instances our interpretation of events and the meaning we give to our views affect how we play out the story of our life over the years.

Let's look at Hillary's story to see the process in action.

When my client Hillary was nine, she and her family returned home after a dinner outing. Immediately, they saw drawers and cupboards ajar. Someone had been in the house. Money was missing. Hillary went downstairs to the TV room and saw a man running out the sliding door. It was a neighbour. When he saw her, he put a finger to his mouth: "*Shhhh.*"

Hillary ran upstairs and told her parents.

They said it couldn't be him. "You are lying, Hillary—never blame someone without knowing the facts."

They didn't believe her, and she felt dismissed.

Unbeknownst to Hillary, she created an interpretation of this episode that her voice no longer mattered.

This became Hillary's story and it affected her for many, many years.

Hillary cruised through high school, letting life just happen, going along for the ride. She grew up a typical girl, with C+ grades. Her mediocre results weren't surprising, because in her world her voice didn't matter—she lacked confidence. She continued to assemble evidence that her judgment was not sound, just as her parents had suggested when she was nine.

Hillary ended up at a second-rate university, giving up a dream she had held as a young child of becoming a lawyer. She superimposed others' ideas and thoughts on her own. She became an observer in her own life and never questioned her story. Over time, Hillary became overwhelmingly warm and friendly, as a way to hide her lack of confidence from others. At age 25, Hillary finally looked at the facts. Yes, she had a mediocre record in high school—but so did many smart and successful people. They went on to do great things because they told themselves a different story, one that drove them to succeed. Perhaps high school marks do not, in fact, predict whether you will be a success. Hillary finally realized that she had given meaning to her own story, and it was not helping her to succeed or to be happy. It was a profound insight for her, one that gave her tremendous power.

Today, Hillary doesn't buy that story any more. She's changed the script. She's taken charge of her life. Now she's living a new story, a far more empowering one.

In a nutshell, Hillary regained her power. I call people like her "power players." And in the next section, we'll look at more examples of how power players like Hillary approach life.

Exercise: Changing your stories.

Now that you have uncovered your truths, challenged your assumptions, and viewed them from different perspectives, you have the entire scope of your story and will be able to see better now what's real, the interpretations you have made, and the meanings you have given certain situations, actions, or reactions.

Write down your "personal truths." You will have uncovered some of these in Power Tool 3: Look at Your Belief System and Personal Truths. Write down all of them, from the easy to the not-so-easy. Continue to dig deep to see what some of those fundamental truths you carry around are. Remember to look at some of the patterns. Do you often find yourself not trusting people? ("People aren't trustworthy.") Are you often jealous or intimidated by others? ("I'm not good enough.") Do you worry about not being smart enough, or people thinking you aren't smart? ("I'm stupid.") Do you have a hard time keeping relationships together? ("I'm not love-able/worthy.") Where did this belief come from and how is it affecting you? Is it still valid? Is it worth keeping around? If it's a big one, and it's getting in your way, there is some work to do to move past it and change it forever. Look in your story to where these were developed so you can choose to change them if they are no longer useful. Since we want to be able to change our stories to make them more empowering, we also need to look at our truths, our beliefs, and our assumptions. This is all the work from the previous power tools now being brought together.

What's my story?	My parents didn't listen to me as a child.
What is my personal truth?	My opinions don't matter. What I say is not worthy of being listened to.
How is it affecting me?	It affects my decisions, my judgments of people and situations, and weakens my self-esteem.
Is this truth worth keeping?	No, it's old and no longer needs to apply.

A blank form to use for **Changing Your Story** is found in the Appendix, on page 152.

Can you see how your story has created your personal truth, which in turn affects what you do or say?

Can you name any examples, big or small, of being affected by a personal truth in the last month?

How does it affect the way you communicate with people? Write down some examples.

What new positive personal truths might you adopt to replace the ones you want to get rid of? What new empowering stories can you use to guide your life? Now that you are seeing how this all comes together, you will be better equipped for the next power tool, "Know you always have a choice."

6
POWER TOOL

Power Tool 6: Know You Always Have a Choice

A big part of gaining or regaining power over your life is opening yourself up to choices, to seeing the options that are available to you. People who give up power often have tunnel vision. They see only one story. Theirs! They are the victim of circumstance, and they are faced with an impossible choice: yes or no. Black or white.

Take my client, Sylvia, who is facing a classic conundrum. She's on the fast track at work, but she's 35, and she wants to have a baby. She wavers. Will she end up on the mommy track, watching her peers move ahead while she gets all the boring work that allows her to get home by 5 p.m.? Or will she have children but stay on the fast track and worry about them, not to mention dealing with those disapproving comments from the other mothers on the edge of the soccer field? Neither option is appealing, and whichever one she chooses is sure to disappoint. She feels like a victim: powerless and doomed to be unhappy because of circumstances beyond her control. She has tunnel vision. And can see only one story: hers.

Unlike those who are feeling like victims, power players think very differently. They recognize their faulty personal truths and assumptions and put them aside, keeping an open mind. They also acknowledge their own limited perspective and work hard to move past it, to see their situation from a broader point of view. Doing this opens them up to other versions of their story, to multiple options and many new possibilities that the victim with tunnel vision didn't even consider.

Let's look again at the woman mulling over having a baby. If she's a power player, she sees multiple options.

- Recognizing that she isn't really going to know how she feels about work and motherhood until after she's been on maternity leave, she could leave the decision until then.

- She could make a choice up front and then review it after every month or two months after the baby arrives (whether she's at home or at work).
- She could make a choice but commit to a time frame for it—for example, she will stay at home until her child turns five, or she will commit to limited hours and a reduced chance for advancement for three years.
- She could choose to stay home altogether and give up her work for the sake of raising her child and possibly children.
- She could discuss flex hours, telecommuting, or part-time work if she were to return to her job.

These are just some of the possibilities that could be available (you might be able to think of many others). The important thing to notice is that the power player is always in action, in conversation with herself. She does not assume there is only one way to see a situation. Her biggest power is her ability to think, to see new openings and other perspectives. What's more, she's prepared to be flexible. Since she sees that there are many possibilities, she can try one, knowing that if it doesn't work for her, there is another option to try next. This revelation gives her a sense of power and control over her destiny—it's incredibly freeing.

Seeing Your Choices

In the power tool above, I described how opening your mind to the possibilities and refusing to think in black and white terms will help you see options. Power Tool 5: View It from a Different Perspective is also a good way to develop a few choices for yourself. Using your "personal values," covered in Chapter 1, is another important technique for trying to see your choices. In fact, reminding yourself of what really makes you tick is a great way to recognize or develop options that are going to work for you. Here's a good illustration of that process:

One of my clients, a senior salesman, came to me with a troubling story. He thought he was about to be fired, and he and his wife had a baby on the way. He didn't like his job, he said. In fact, he didn't like sales at all. That was the problem in his previous five jobs. They just didn't fit his skills or make him happy. He didn't see himself as a salesman. He had to visit the company's existing clients once a week, and all he could think about was what he was going to try to sell them. He had a very narrow definition of what sales was.

"So," I asked, "what do you love to do?"

His reply: "I love to be creative, I love to have fun, and I need excitement."

"So how can you have that in your job?" I asked.

We started to talk about how he could expand his definition of sales. He changed his approach to include some of his needs. He started building relationships with his clients over beers and lunch. He got to know them as human beings. He took responsibility for his lax behaviour of the past and even wrote to a client whom he had disappointed.

Then he looked inside himself and realized that picking up the phone to call a client paralyzed him. *Why would they want to talk to me?* He was worried about what the person on the other end of the line would think. We worked together on the story he told himself about himself, and along the way he realized that he was standing in his own way. If he changed his view of himself, and of his role as a salesman, and the definition of sales that he had made up, he would shine.

And he did. He became the company's top salesman.

There are a number of ways to develop or to see what options really exist for you. Many of these methods require some sustained attention and self-reflection. Does that mean that you should never make a visceral decision? Does seeing all of your choices mean that you should never follow your gut? Not at all. Sometimes our intuitive responses and visceral choices are really good ones—reactions that are no doubt tapping into some deep, unconscious knowledge of ourselves. If you have a gut feeling about a choice, go ahead, follow that. But just keep in mind that if it doesn't seem to be working out, you need to look at the other options available to you and make a change.

Exercise: Seeing your choices.

Write down a problem or a situation you are struggling with. Come up with three or more possible solutions. It's important that you create at least three options, as opposed to two—having only two makes it black or white, right or wrong. There is a loss of freedom in having only two options because the one not chosen seems to always hang around, making you feel regretful or that you made the wrong choice.

An example follows:

Situation	Unhappy at work
Choice 1	Suck it up
Choice 2	Quit
Choice 3	Stay and see if I can move within the company
Choice 4	Stay but look for another job
Choice 5	Stay and get coaching or a mentor
Choice 6	Accept responsibility for my mindset and recommit to the company

A blank form to use for **Power Tool 6: Know You Always Have a Choice** is found in the Appendix, on page 153.

This exercise will help you to visualize that your original option is not the only choice, and may not even be the best one.

Just reminding yourself of your choices and asking these questions will open up new possibilities for you, no matter what your situation.

Regaining Power: A Seven-Point Checklist

1. You always have a choice, always.
2. Stop talking about "them"; focus on you. What can you do?
3. The past is the past; what counts is how you are right now.
4. Is your story true? Are you reacting to something that didn't happen?
5. Are your personal truths and assumptions constraining you?
6. Is it possible you are reacting this way because you have a misconstrued belief?
7. What choices might address your personal values?

Victim or Power Player?

At the end of Chapter 2, I asked if you might be feeling or acting like a victim. And in the previous pages of this chapter, I suggested that you could use a number of techniques and power tools to move past a victim approach, such as focusing on you; taking responsibility; checking your personal truths, assumptions, and perspectives; adjusting your stories; and thinking about your options. These are what power players, those who have taken control of their lives, do.

As you work on regaining your power, it's always a good idea to check your progress—to see if you are indeed moving from victim to power player. The process starts inside your head. The power player always begins with a simple premise: It's up to me. As a power player, you have the ability to choose what happens in your life, and how you react to a situation. You do not blame other people for what happens to you. You know you always have a very significant power—the ability to choose how you view a situation. You gain considerable leeway by separating fact from fiction, so that you are reacting to the bare facts, not to the story you have fabricated about the facts, a story that may be based on your personal truths and assumptions and the stories rooted in your personal history. You then scope out plenty of options, not just two uninspiring ones.

Read through the following examples with an eye to whether the victim or the power player sounds like you.

The victim: Why do I always end up with these people (insert employees, bosses, friends)?

The power player: What am I doing or saying to put myself into this situation? Why did I choose those friends, that job, and how can I make better choices next time?

What can I do to take responsibility for this outcome and change it? What is it about me that is creating this result? (If the same result occurs more than once, you need to look at the common denominator: you. *Am I too righteous, do I listen, am I authentic?*)

See how this victim is always also blaming others? The power player asks herself how she got into this situation and how she can change her strategy or perspective on people to make better choices. She's not happy about it, but at least she can do something and move on.

The victim: They don't listen to me. They never do.

The power player: I can see my message isn't getting through, so how can I speak so they listen? Then again, if they don't listen, maybe it's their problem. They can live with the consequences. Sometimes they have to fail in order to learn. It's my choice: Go in for the save, or let them mess up.

Look at the victim. It doesn't really matter whether she's talking about her employees or the kids. *They don't listen to me. It's their fault.* She can't think of anything she can do to make the employees/children listen. You can almost hear the whine in her voice. Did you ever notice that it's often the same person who makes this type of complaint at work and at home?

The power player is in action. She asks what she can do to get the message through. There could be lots of reasons why they are not listening. Maybe she has to fine-tune her message and the way she delivers it to the audience at hand. Even if that's not possible, she knows she still has a decision to make; let them fail and learn from mistakes, go in for the save, coach them, or fire them.

The victim: Why is she always so rude to me?

The power player: I value your friendship, but I need to tell you something. What you said angers me. That's not okay behaviour. You can't treat me like that. Am I doing or behaving in a way that offends you and is that why you're treating me rudely?

The victim is in pain. She feels diminished, humiliated. But she is failing to see that she is in charge of who is in her life, and how she is treated. If she lets people treat her badly, that's what they will do. By saying nothing directly to the friend, she's giving up her power, teaching that person that the behaviour is acceptable. The power player, in contrast, acts proactively to draw the line.

The victim: I hate my job but I can't afford to leave it. I have to support my family, send my kids to private schools, and keep up the cottage. So I'm stuck.

The power player: I have a choice. I can sell my cottage, send the kids to public school, live a simpler life, and do something I like to do. Or I can make a choice that for now, my lifestyle is more important than my satisfaction at work. I can always look for something else at the same time.

The victim is stuck because she's not seeing that she made a choice to live in a certain way. She has tunnel vision and doesn't see her options. Maintaining her family lifestyle is not the only choice, but if she chooses to have it, then she should acknowledge she's made that choice.

The victim: The managers are idiots, so it's no surprise they made such a stupid decision. If I were in charge, it would all be different.

The power player: That's an interesting thing they did. I wonder what problems they were trying to address with this decision?

The victim is frustrated, but her anger comes from seeing the situation from only her point of view. She doesn't know anything about the challenges her bosses are facing, but she complains anyway. The power player accepts the idea that there are different perspectives and that she can't see everything that the managers are dealing with.

While anyone can feel or behave like a victim, there are three situations in which women often end up adopting the victim mantle: romantic relationships, motherhood, and divorce. Let's spend a bit of time looking at each of these.

Romance: Victims and Power Players

How many of you have put the future of your relationship in the hands of the guy you're dating? You don't ask "Where is this going?" for fear of him saying "I'm just happy with the way things are right now." You're afraid to bring up the question of monogamy in case he responds by saying he's not really interested in a committed relationship. You don't bring up marriage in case he runs for the hills. Now when you are in this place, how is the relationship? Fulfilling, easy, peaceful, free? Unlikely. In this situation, do you feel you can be who you are or act the way you want? I bet not.

Women tend to hand over their power in the relationship very quickly, and it's hard to get it back. All too often we allow the man to set the tone and pace of the relationship, and we go along, even when we're unhappy.

As mentioned earlier, most women are bonders and want to connect and find a companion. In order to create that bond and connection, women tend to take the cues from men. They'll compromise or even sell out for that outcome.

This need to bond can go too far. Have you ever lost yourself in your relationship? Have you given up your friends, your interests, and your commitments only to take on his? This is handing over your power. As time goes on, women feel unsatisfied, undervalued, unappreciated, and helpless. Yet more often than not, the woman stays in the relationship and struggles. In essence, she has turned herself into a victim.

If you're in this situation, what should you do? How do you change yourself into a power player? First, accept that he is who he is. There is no power in trying to change that or what he wants or what he does. The power is in accepting him for exactly who he is—the good, the bad, and the ugly.

Take responsibility for being the one who has handed the control of your happiness over to him. It's time to take back your life, and take back your power. Look inside yourself for your power. What do you need, and what do you want in a man, in a relationship? Does he fit into your world? To answer that question, I have clients make a list of all the qualities they want in a partner. Then they divide that list into three columns. One is "Everything I Want." The second is "I Could Live Without," and the third is the "Deal Breakers"—the "I have to have it or forget it." Then I ask clients compare to that list to the lists they've already made of fill-me-ups and personal values. When they compare the lists, they often find they have to rejig their wish list a little.

Once you've made your wish list, you can ask yourself this question: Is your boyfriend or husband the right person for you? You have the power after all. You can choose to stay—or walk. If you choose to stay, despite the problems, you're making a powerful choice.

Knowing you have a choice can give you a fresh perspective on your partner, even if you don't do anything dramatic. One of my clients complained that her husband was a neat freak who liked to go out far more often than she did. He'd come home, complain about the mess, and then angle to go out, with or without her. She longed to change him so that he would be more relaxed, be at home more, and be more communicative with her at the dinner table. But he wasn't changing, so she was getting increasingly angry and frustrated.

First, we worked on acceptance. He's a neat freak, and he wasn't going to change. But that didn't mean she had to become a neat freak too. So when he'd come home and complain, she would say to herself, *Oh well, that's your perspective, not mine.* She didn't let the neat freak complaints bother her. If he was upset by a little mess, he could clean it up himself. Next, she accepted that he liked to go out. She chose him, after all, for many reasons including his sociable personality. So now he goes out and she often stays in, but she makes dates for them to stay home for a cosy dinner—and puts it in his calendar. These simple attitude adjustments have moved her from the victim role to the power player role—and she now feels great about herself and her relationship.

Motherhood: Victims and Power Players

There is more than one route from motherhood to the victim zone, believe me. Let's take a look at how three women got there.

Sharon blames her lack of motivation, lack of self-esteem, and lack of mojo, on motherhood. When she was pregnant, she and her husband decided she would give up her career to stay home and raise her kids. That was fine at first, but as the kids grew up and signed up for sports and other activities, Sharon spent most of her time taxi driving, doing the laundry, organizing the family, and cooking meals. Now she feels resentful at the end of the day; there's no joy in her life. She loves her kids, but she feels she has no skills to re-enter the workforce. She feels like she has nothing to offer the world.

Another client, Julie, has become a victim in a different way. It involves her daughter Mary. She is not studying, is too social and irresponsible, and doesn't seem to care about her future. Mary is in the last years of high school, but she doesn't believe that she needs to study hard for the marks to get into university. My client feels completely powerless. She can't help her daughter avoid mistakes that could affect the rest of her life.

And a third client, Martha, fell into victimhood when facing the challenges of combining paid work and motherhood. She says she's been passed over for a promotion because her boss thinks she is more committed to the kids than to the job. She's furious. After all, when her husband stays late at work, he just calls home and says, "Honey, I'm staying late at work, I'll be home later." If Martha wants to stay late at work, she has to figure out how to get the kids home from school, who will drive them to soccer practice, and whether her sitter can come over for a few hours and cook dinner—if there's something frozen in the fridge. She's trying to work out the details of the childcare during a meeting, so she's not really paying attention to what the vice-president of marketing is saying. At the end of the day, Martha feels as though she hasn't delivered on either job she's doing. She goes home feeling guilty, frustrated, and torn.

Walking away from the job or the kids obviously isn't a choice she's willing to consider, so Martha starts blaming her husband: "He doesn't have to make a choice, so why should I? Why is all this on my shoulders?"

All three of these mothers are blaming their unhappiness and frustration on their circumstances. Although their circumstances are different, the way out, the path to turning themselves from victims to power players, starts with the same question: What can I do?

What do you actually control? Julie, for instance, cannot control her daughter Mary. She cannot force Mary to do her homework. She can state her opinion—university is an important launching pad—but whether or not Mary goes there will be Mary's decision. Mary will have to live with the consequences. It might help if Julie showed her confidence in Mary.

She can tell Mary that she's confident that Mary will be able to handle the outcome, however it turns out. Standing by while Mary makes an important choice is not easy, but it's crucial. It's the only way Mary will learn. And what's more, it means that Mary is exercising the power she has.

Sharon thinks she has nothing to offer, but is that true? If Sharon drops the personal truths and negative stories she's been telling herself, she might escape her tunnel vision. With a power-player approach, Sharon could come up with a list of options for herself. Perhaps she could find a part-time job that would give her enough income to pay someone else to clean her house or do her grocery shopping. Maybe she can have her children pick up some of the domestic chores and develop their independence so she has more time for fill-me-up activities that will make the rest of her routine more bearable. Or perhaps she could take online or night courses to upgrade her skills, which will prepare her to re-enter the paid workforce at some point.

And what can Martha do to stop struggling under the double load of work and family, and get out of the victim zone?

First, she has to take responsibility for her choice to work and to have a family. This choice was never going to make for an easy life, which she knew when she took it on.

Next, she needs to look at her assumptions and expectations. If she's blaming her spouse for not sharing the load, did she just assume it would be a 50-50 split on childcare and housework? Did she discuss this with her husband in advance? Did he agree? Or did she assume that women are supposed to do everything, or that moms are better at being with the kids? Did she, for instance, act out these assumptions when her children were babies? When you start blaming, always look at yourself first. What role did you play?

Once Martha has taken responsibility for her choices, she can consider her options. She might try using Power Tool 5: View It from a Different Perspective to make sure she is considering a wide array of options, not just a couple. For example, would she consider setting up her own consulting business instead of working in a large corporation? She may also find that her company can offer talented women like her a more flexible work plan than the old-fashioned 9 to 5. She might be surprised how open her company is—the Millennials, after all, are asking for the same thing. If that option isn't available, she could look at other companies that do offer it.

Once she's looked at all the options, she can make a choice. Or she can decide not to change. Either way, she has her power back and is now living like a power player, not a victim.

Divorce: Victims and Power Players

Divorce can easily send both men and women to the victim zone. I hear it all the time from my clients. The husband isn't paying his child support or is paying late. He doesn't turn up on time to pick up the kids on the weekend or doesn't show up at all. When he does see the kids, he plays Mr. Nice Guy and undermines the discipline my clients are trying to impose in the home.

Women who make these kinds of complaints have no power. The ex-husband is pulling all the strings. Even if it's true that their ex-husbands are causing the problems, it doesn't help them move forward. The complaints just turn them into a victim. And if they keep complaining, they'll get more stuck and angry over time.

One of my clients has an ex-husband who spends very little time with their daughter. He misses dates with his daughter, he is late for outings, and he changes his scheduled weekends constantly. Their son lives with him. He spoils their son and doesn't take any responsibility for him at all. Now their son is getting into trouble and is failing in school. The ex is also trying to avoid paying the full amount of spousal and child support.

What can my client do? Well, the first step is realizing that she can't change her ex. Perhaps this is exactly why he is an ex. And she can adopt a power player's position: concentrating on herself and her relationship with her children—what she can do and how she can think and behave. She can remind herself she's a great parent committed to a particular way of living and parenting. (Parents in this situation are often extremely committed to their children and to ensuring they are okay.) She may choose to teach her children some of the power tools from this book. She can help her daughter manage her expectations. Or she can develop ways to help her daughter find power in a disappointing situation. Perhaps she can work on ways to connect with her son so she has more influence on his behaviour. What else would a power player do in this situation? She would change her reactions, or her perspective. She can discuss other options with her ex or she can also decide whether to take him to court to regain the full amount of money he owes her.

She may have to pick her battles, but the point is that she is making choices for herself and her family. By making choices, she'll be operating from a place of power, not from a pit of anger and desperation.

In all these cases, the difference between power players and victims is how they view the situation, how they think, and how they react. And the move from victim to power player can be as simple as realizing this: You always have choices.

Exercise: Who do you want to be today?

We've talked about transforming yourself from a victim to a power player, but sometimes we don't need to make journeys that are that significant. Sometimes we are just looking to improve ourselves in small ways (something power players do all the time). Here's a great exercise to help you make those changes.

Ask yourself this question: What kind of person do I want to be today?

Being that person, what thoughts would I have?

What behaviours would I exhibit, what physical sensations would I experience?

Say, for example, you'd like to be more outgoing. What does an outgoing person look like? Does she smile? Does she use her hands when she talks? Does she use other forms of body language? How close does she stand to other people?

When you have this picture very specifically in your mind, you can then start to take on some of these attributes and behaviours in your life. As they say, "Fake it until you make it."

This exercise is particularly helpful when you take on a new job at work. One of my clients, Caitlin, was promoted to a management position. Now she had to supervise her friends. How would she do it?

She started by asking these questions: *What kind of person do I want to be in this role? What kind of people are successful in this role, and what's necessary for success? What kind of manager do I admire, and how can I learn from him or her? How can I incorporate some of his or her behaviours or practices into my own work?*

In her new job as director of sales, she knew she had to be accountable for the numbers. But she wanted to be more than that. She wanted to be a boss who inspires people to be successful. If her employees were successful, she would be too.

To do this, she knew she had to move from a friendship relationship with her staff to a boss relationship. So she held one-on-one meetings with her work friends to tell them how the office would run from now on. She visualized how she would look, how she would move and carry herself, even what clothes she would wear. She acted the way a boss would act and no longer as a peer would act.

It worked: She became the person she imagined, and everyone respected her and her new position instead of resenting her for it.

Visualization is tremendously effective. As most high-performance athletes know, the key to visualization is to really feel it. You have to feel the physical and emotional sensation for it to sink in. You have to experience it in your brain, so your brain believes that it is real. That way when you engage in that athletic sport, or movement, or behaviour, your brain already knows what to do. Affirm this new image of yourself throughout the day, and soon you won't have to. Your brain will know what to do.

7
POWER TOOL

Power Tool 7: Affirm Yourself in a Positive Way—Every Day

The concept behind affirmations is to rewire your brain from the negative thoughts to positive. Tell yourself many times a day "I am strong" or "I can handle it" or "I am worthy of love, success, happiness." Before you know it, your brain will relate to this as the way you are. This may seem unrealistic to you, especially if you're the kind of person who thinks, *I can't do it, I'm not good enough* or *Why would anybody believe me?* That's insecurity talking, and it's made up. By you. You are the one who says you are not good enough, not worthy, not up to snuff. Even if others have told you this it doesn't make it true. The only thing that counts is what you say about yourself. So reframe your opinion of yourself. You are the one who sets the image of you. Then others will believe what you believe.

Make a list of all your negative truths. Going back to Power Tool 3: Look at Your Belief System and Personal Truths will give you some context and examples of typical personal truths that we carry around with us. If you look at the situations or people who trigger certain reactions in you, you will have an opening for seeing what some of these truths might be. Write down the opposite of this truth as an affirmation about yourself.

What triggers me?	When people are late.
What is the personal truth creating that reaction?	I'm not worthy because people think my time is not valuable.
What is the affirmation that combats that truth?	I am worthy of all that is good in the world.

A blank form to use for **Power Tool 7: Affirm Yourself in a Positive Way Every Day** is found in the Appendix, on page 153.

When you have negative thoughts, consciously replace them with positive ones. This will train your brain to stop calling on negative thoughts to respond to a situation and instead call upon positive ones. Another exercise you can do in the moment of being triggered is say or think "Stop" and put your hand up. Your hand will distract your brain from the current thought so you can replace it with a positive thought or affirmation. You will be surprised how quickly this works and how even the most obsessive, irrational thoughts will become a part of your past.

8
POWER TOOL

Power Tool 8: Forgive, Learn Your Lesson, and Move On

I used to think that forgiveness meant condoning the bad behaviour, but now I see it differently. When you forgive, you are not saying, *That was good behaviour, good for you.*

Instead, I say this:

What you did was not okay by me. Yet holding on to that anger only affects me, no one else. In fact, by staying angry, I'm only handing over my power to the person who hurt me. So I may not agree with the behaviour, the actions, the words, but I need to forgive so that I can move on in a powerful way.

Here are a few practical tips to help you forgive:

- Remember that you have no control over the other person. What did he do? It was wrong in your books, but in his world that was the thing to do. It's not okay with you, but you can't change it.
- Learn that those who victimize are sad human beings. These are not powerful people. They are people who like to be in control. Seeing them as sad people who cannot thrive without victims will help you to put them into perspective. You might even learn to laugh about their failings.
- Then look at yourself and consider what you got from this bad behaviour: *I'm a different person because of that,* or *I've learned a lesson and I appreciate that.*

That insight will help you move forward. I have a client who, many years ago, had a tenant who neglected to pay a $1,000 bill for a rented apartment. The anger he felt has stayed with him for years. However, since he became an entrepreneur, he has set up his business to make sure his clients pay their bills on time. That $1,000 unpaid bill taught him a huge lesson that he has applied in his business and may in fact be saving him thousands of dollars more. Acknowledging that the pent-up anger was affecting only him and no one else allowed my client to move past the negative emotions and be able to see the lessons that he learned from this betrayal and the blessing that experience really was.

It's not easy to forgive someone, but it's mandatory to move on. It's the only way to loosen the grip of anger that is choking you.

Here is an example of how this works.

Individuals or situations I feel are unresolved	Paul Smith
Emotions I am holding on to	Betrayal, anger
What do I need to forgive them or myself for?	Not paying the rent on the apartment, causing me to have to cover that expense
What is the lesson to be learned?	1. Always have iron-clad contracts 2. Receive payments up front

A blank form to use for **Power Tool 8: Forgive, Learn Your Lesson, and Move On** is found in the Appendix, on page 154.

Forgiving yourself is even harder, because you have to take responsibility for your actions and the impact you've had on people. How do you do it? Perhaps you can write yourself a letter. Acknowledge the facts and what you've done. No excuses. Be honest about the impact your actions had on other people. What do you know about how they felt? Imagine what it would be like on their side. Recognize you can't change what you've done.

Now, do you have apologies to make? Look in the mirror and forgive yourself. Apologize to yourself in the mirror. Say, *I forgive you.*

You may have to forgive yourself for not standing up for yourself, for selling out on yourself.

Remember, when something happens that you don't like, you can't change it, but you can learn a lesson. Keep the lesson, not the anger and resentment. In other words, move on in whichever powerful way you choose.

9
POWER TOOL

Power Tool 9: Don't Tolerate. Accept

Look at how you are right now, and ask yourself this question:

What would it be like if nothing changed?

This question might surprise you, especially if you're seeking to change yourself. But to change, first you have to get real about what's out there. Maybe your boss does favour his golfing buddies. Maybe your spouse doesn't love you any more and is sticking around just for the kids. Maybe you did lose a bundle in the market.

What if that is the situation, and it won't change? Would you be okay with that?

If the answer is yes, that clear view of reality, and your decision to accept your situation, puts you in the power seat. If the answer is no, ask yourself what you are going to do next.

You will have power because you're acting on the basis of your reality, not the way you'd like it to be.

Most people think acceptance is tolerance, but tolerance comes with resentment. Why? Because you tolerate it, you are in essence putting up with it. There is a judgment that it's not okay but you can't do anything about it. You are not at peace with it, you continually ruminate about it over and over, and it doesn't go away. When you accept it, you are at peace, and it dissipates.

One of my clients, Nicola, kept complaining about her marriage. The spark had gone out of it, but despite everything that Nicola was doing to introduce a little more romance into her relationship, nothing she was trying seemed to revitalize their less-than-frequent love life. She had said early on in our discussions that she had accepted this state of affairs—that she was taking the good of her marriage with the bad. But Nicola was tolerating her husband's behaviour, not accepting it. And because of that, she was continuing to be frustrated and annoyed every time her husband did not respond the way she wanted him to.

We worked on this over a few sessions. First, Nicola had to give up her hope that her husband would change. Then we looked at all of Nicola's options. Walking away from her marriage was not one of the choices she was going to opt for at this time. Since couples counselling was not something her husband would agree to participate in, she chose to embrace her marriage just the way it was. She worked hard at truly accepting the state of her love life, and that finally allowed her to genuinely enjoy all that was good in the relationship.

You can also gain power by accepting someone else's point of view.

Take my client Jenny, who thinks her boss is wrong. That's all she can see. He's a bully. Everything the boss says or does is filtered through that lens. On the other hand if she can accept that her boss can be unnecessarily difficult on occasion, she can say, "Oh yeah, he can do that sometimes and this is one of those times." Yet she can also see that the boss has other facets of his character, and some of them are well suited to his position. This gives Jenny power because she's no longer trapped by her resentment toward her boss and she doesn't waste countless hours complaining. Instead, she can use all that free time to get on with her work and do the best she can.

When you don't accept other people, you operate as if they are wrong, yielding criticism, cynicism, and blame. When you're blaming, you have no power. You don't think, *How could I do better?*

If you let people be who they are and genuinely accept them, you free up energy and power because you're not trying to control them or fix them. You can spend that energy on productive endeavours that you can control.

The following is an example:

Traits of individuals in my life or my circumstances that I wish I could change	I wish my boss was not such a bully.
Do I acknowledge I cannot change this?	I realize I cannot change him.
Declare that I accept it by either sharing it with the individual or writing it down	I will write down in my journal that I accept him and his behaviours just as they are right now.

A blank form to use for **Power Tool 9: Don't Tolerate. Accept** is found in the Appendix, on page 154.

You now have nine power tools to implement "The YOU Factor."

Power Tool 1: Accept responsibility
Power Tool 2: Check your story
Power Tool 3: Look at your belief system and personal truths
Power Tool 4: Challenge your assumptions
Power Tool 5: View it from a different perspective
Power Tool 6: Know you always have a choice
Power Tool 7: Affirm yourself in a positive way—every day
Power Tool 8: Forgive, learn your lesson, and move on
Power Tool 9: Don't tolerate. Accept

It requires practice to automatically use these power tools, particularly given how we can default back to our automatic ways of being when we're facing a stressful fight-or-flight situation. In time, though, it can just be like riding a bicycle—once you've learned, you never forget.

Once on the bike, beware of the potholes! These potholes are what I call traps, discussed in the next chapter.

4

Beware of the Traps

Trapped by the Past: Assuming That History Repeats Itself

As we've seen, the past can spring a lot of traps. We can tell ourselves stories about what happened in the past, which become the stories that affect how we act and think today. But this one is different: People think the past will repeat itself in the future, so they act today as if the past will repeat itself tomorrow. In essence, they put their past in their future.

Let's look at some examples of how this works.

Take my client Ella, who has been spurned by her boyfriend: That's just how men are, she says. They can't commit. Yet this is a trap. It's not true that everyone, or even every man, can't commit. That's just her experience. Is it possible she feels that way because she chooses men like that, men who can't commit? Of course, she doesn't think of it that way—she blames the men she's dated in the past. So guess what happens? She doesn't look for signs that a man might be able to commit; she overlooks the men who can. She goes out and finds another man just like the ones she's dated in the past. It only confirms her belief that the future is just like the past. And she gets to be righteous about it.

What she doesn't realize is this: If she changes the way she operates—and chooses different kinds of men—perhaps the future will be different.

THE TRAP: Believing that something will lead to an already assumed outcome. If this isn't an outcome you want, change your belief.

EXAMPLE:
Belief: In my last job, my boss let me sink or swim. It's no use asking for help in my new job.
Outcome: I didn't ask for advice when I really needed it, and I made a big mistake.

UNLOCK THE TRAP:
Change your belief: There are people who will help me if I need it. Belief guides action: I find co-workers who can give me useful guidance.
Outcome: I finish my task successfully.

I'm not suggesting here that you do not learn from experience. You may approach new relationships or new clients with a certain amount of caution, given what you've learned from the past. But never assume that everyone you meet will treat you poorly.

Exercise: Separating past, present, and future.
Look at all the areas in your life. Where have you put the past into your future? Imagine your memory is divided into three parts: the past, the present, and the future.

Past   Present   Future

Now imagine that the past box is full of all your past experiences. They are done and over with. The present box is filling up as the day goes on so it's a little full, and the future—well, it hasn't happened yet so it's empty of any experiences. Now imagine that you are moving your past box into storage, but instead of dropping it in the storage area you accidentally drop it into the future box. Now the future box is no longer empty but full of all the past experiences. So every time something happens in the present, you can see it in the future, and you live like that's what will happen. You are constantly reliving the past. That's why the same events and patterns happen over and over. So you need to go and take that past box out of the future box and put it in storage because the future has not happened yet. You don't know what will happen. The future box is empty! Now, look at all the times you say, "Oh I know exactly what he will say," or "I know what she will do," or "I know how they will react" and then see what it would be like if you actually didn't know. How would you react? What would you say? What would you do? What might be different?

Trapped by the Future: Your Expectations

It's not just the past that can trap us. We can lose power if we have expectations for the future.

This may seem odd. Isn't it a good thing to have a target, a goal? Isn't that a prime motivator? It is, but a goal is very different from an expectation.

A goal you work toward. You want it, you strive for it, you prepare for it. You are always in action, making it happen. That is a power player position.

An expectation is quite different. It's a belief about what will happen in the future, and it's generated by your personal truth and assumptions—the way things are. Expectations, unlike goals, rob you of power. Why? You expect something to happen, but you're not doing anything to make it happen. It is, therefore, out of your control. And you have become a victim. An unmet expectation *always* ends in disappointment.

For example, you expect him to propose on Valentine's Day, and then you wait for it to happen. But the actual proposal is not in your control. You are powerless and disappointed if your expectation is not met. You've just given your power to that expectation.

This happens on the job all the time. People think the job should meet their expectations, so they don't bring everything they have to their work. They wait for the job and the people in the company to meet their expectations.

Here's an example: You had a great year last year at work. You had a plan; you achieved your goals. This year you want a promotion. You expect it because of last year's performance.

You believe that last year's performance will carry you through this year, so you've adopted a more comfortable mindset. You are less focused on this year's performance. You're coasting.

Then you fumble a couple of times. The promotion goes to a colleague, not you.

You stopped striving for the promotion. You started expecting it.

The problem with an expectation is that you stop pushing yourself. You take yourself out of the game. You're not going all out. You give up taking responsibility for how your life turns out and hand that power over to someone else.

Let's go back to the reluctant salesman we met when we were talking about values and choices. He becomes the top sales guy in his company by changing the kind of salesperson he wanted to be. He focuses on building relationships, being creative, and gaining confidence with the phone calls and personal meetings. But now he's fixing his eye on the target, the numbers. With two weeks to go, it doesn't look as though he's going to make his numbers. He's still short by 1%. He starts approaching clients in a different way. It's all about the numbers, and they know it. "People aren't returning my calls," he tells me. "I'm having a hard time closing the numbers gap."

The problem: He had an expectation that hitting his numbers would be no problem and that his clients would come through to ensure that. He was now focusing on his expectation of meeting numbers. The numbers ruled, and all that he had learned went down the drain. He was giving over his power to the numbers and his clients.

When we saw this, he went back to his successful approach—focusing on the personal qualities of the person he wanted to be. He regained power.

No, he didn't make his numbers that year, but at least he had regained the power to move forward and succeed next year. He didn't blame his clients for not helping him or keeping their promises. He didn't blame himself for not reaching the goal. He focused on his accomplishments and what he needed to know to meet and exceed the goal the next year.

I talked earlier about the risk of cruising along when you expect something rather than working to make it happen, but the salesman's experience illustrates another way expectations can trip you up. You can still work extremely hard for something, but if you expect results that are truly outside of your control, you are likely to be frustrated. But working without the expectations, just as my client learned to do, reaps all sorts of rewards, without delivering crushing disappointment when the expectations aren't met.

Expectations can rob you of not only power but joy in your everyday life. Say you go on a trip to Africa, and you expect to see lions, giraffes, and zebras on safari. You spend all your time looking for the animals, and if you don't see them, you're disappointed. You have paid to see animals, and you have a guide to help find them, but what if you don't get to see any? It's like going fishing and not catching anything. You are putting all your happiness and enjoyment into the hands of the animals or the guide. Although he's experienced, does he have power over the animals? Of course not.

Or it's Saturday and the weather report said it was going to be sunny. The weather report, once again, was wrong. It's raining. You're annoyed at missing your golf game and you stew all day. The power of expectations ruined the first part of your weekend. If you forget about your expectations and live the day, you might have moments to remember, like a wet walk in the woods with your child, and the chance to put your face up to the sky and feel the rain streaming down your face.

People ruled by expectations will often say "You should" or "You shouldn't." They're setting up an expectation, and chances are, they'll be disappointed. Nothing lives up to their expectations—not the weather, or the play last night, or the menu at the restaurant. They're comparing real life—with the sudden traffic jam and the flowers that don't bloom on time—with an expectation they created. In doing so, without realizing it, they've just handed power over the joy of their life to that expectation.

Exercise: Managing your expectations.

What are some of your expectations?
How are those expectations affecting you and others?
Are those expectations realistic? Perhaps they need to be reassessed.

Expectation	That my boyfriend would propose on Valentine's Day.
Outcome when not met	I feel disappointed, frustrated, and unloved.
Relationship with others/self/situation	I'm mad at my boyfriend, feel selfish, and am not expressing myself because I don't want him to know what I was expecting.
Realistic?	It may have been realistic but if I was waiting for him, then I have no say when the engagement will happen. If it's not happening in my time frame, then I need to regain my power and make choices for my future according to what I want and need.

Avoiding a Decision

Let's be really straight here. Not making a choice is making a choice. It's making a choice to leave your fate up to the universe, God, the other person, your circumstances, or destiny. We often cover up our choice avoidance by saying, *I don't know what to do; what if I make the wrong choice?* You sit in limbo and tell yourself, *It's not my fault.* You may even be waiting for someone or something to make the decision for you, or for circumstances to change so that you no longer have to make a decision or you can make one that is less uncomfortable. Sound familiar? How much power do you feel you have when you are in limbo? None. When you are in one place, you are thinking perhaps the other side would be better. And when you are in the other place, you are thinking of the opposite side again. You don't have any power. All you're doing is waiting.

The Quick Fix

I'm not happy, so I'll have an affair.
I'm not happy, so I'm quitting.
I'm not happy, so I'll move to New York.

This is the quick fix. It looks like you're taking dramatic action to make yourself happier and more fulfilled, but in fact you are only reacting to an unhappy situation by looking for someone or something to make you happy.

You are doing something all right, but your action is not thought out. It's a quick reaction to your circumstances.

We like quick. We expect our lives to be as speedy as a Google search. But if you have a romantic fling or move to a different city, guess what? You've addressed the symptom, not the cause. Nothing has fundamentally changed; you are still the same person. Chances are, you'll soon find yourself in the same position in the next marriage or city. Nothing will change because you haven't changed. All you've done is put expectations on another person, job, or city to make you happy. And those expectations are bigger because you've treated the symptom believing you have treated the cause.

For starters, you haven't taken responsibility for yourself or for the outcome of your decisions. Say you leave your husband for another man. You expected your spouse to make you happy and he didn't, so you bolted. Now you expect your new lover to make you happy, and if he doesn't, what will you do? Get another one?

Take one executive I know. He left his wife for another woman. He's the third lover this woman has had during her marriage, and this time she left her husband. Now after a year of dating, the executive is worried she's not in it for the long term. She won't commit. His self-esteem has gone down. Every time she goes away on a trip he's anxious. He's afraid she will find someone else. Just like she has done in the past.

Hmmm... He has just added the "fear trap" to the "quick fix trap" he fell into earlier. Both are now keeping him from having any power.

He is run by his fear that she will leave him. Since she has had many affairs, she might just have one on him. This perhaps could be true. He won't know until that day comes. But the day will come sooner with his fears and insecurities getting in the way. To regain power he must either commit 100% and let the future happen as it may or possibly listen to his fears and leave. Taking complete responsibility of the facts of the relationship and how it came to be is the first step. The quick fix is layered between expectations and possible fears.

It's the same story in your job. If you expect your job to make you happy and it doesn't, you might jump to another company. But now you will be expecting the new job to make you happy. Yet if you don't take responsibility for the only part you control, for yourself, for your own happiness and fulfillment in your job or your marriage, how is that supposed to happen?

The quick fix trap can lead to being a serial husband or a serial employee.

If you're in this position, stop. You've missed the first few steps. Go back to the beginning of this book, and start by assuming responsibility for yourself. Take it step by step from there. Look at your options, and make your choice based on your deep values and priorities. Then, if you still want to leave, do it. It may hurt, and it probably will, but at least it will be a powerful choice, and you will be less likely to regret it.

The Words You Use

Action starts with the words. The words you use to interpret an event affect the way you feel and how you react. So consider the words you use.

Writers choose words carefully. So can you.

Say you're stuck in a job you hate.

If you say *I can't leave my job,* you instantly feel deflated, stuck. No wonder: You've given up all your power. You're resigning yourself to many unhappy days at work. You'll be resentful and frustrated every day.

I can't is such a powerless phrase. Those words tell your brain you aren't capable, that you have no choice. But the fact is, you can. You are able. No one is stopping you from moving to London, or changing jobs, or trying something new—except you.

If, on the other hand, you say, *I choose to keep this job,* look at the difference. Just using the word "choose" is telling yourself that you are able. Even if your job hasn't changed yet, your attitude toward it has. You have made your choice; you have gained the power. Now, if you choose, you can make changes to improve your job, or just live with it and know why you're doing it.

(Be careful here, though. If you are thinking, *Really, what other choice do I have?* you have no power. You're giving it up to circumstances or to someone else, and you will still feel the tinges of anger and resentment.)

So, when speaking or even thinking about your life, avoid words that emphasize a loss of power:

can't

have to

need to

always

never

problem

made me

should

shouldn't

must

and especially,

yeah but

Yeah but is one of the clearest signs that you are being negative and close-minded. It may sound like you are agreeing, but you are dismissing any positive notions.

You could quit your job.

Yeah but ... I have all these bills to pay, and I have a family to support.

You could get another job.

Yeah but ... Where else would I work? The economy is slow, and no one is hiring.

You could do something else.

Yeah but ... What would I do? Where would I go?

You could go back to school and get trained for a job in demand.

Yeah but ...

The issue is not whether the justifications are good. Of course we want to be responsible and take care of our families. The issue is how the *yeah buts* affect you. Do they leave you in a place of power, control, and happiness? Or are they leaving you feeling like a victim—unhappy, resentful, resigned, and powerless? Those words keep you in the victim mindset because you dismiss any choices or possible actions that move you toward power.

When you find yourself using negative words, choose instead words that are empowering:

can   able

will   choose

Who Are You Trying to Control?

When we talk about control, we usually mean one thing: control over other people. You control your employees' activities. You tell your children what to do and hopefully they do it.

But that's not what I mean when I talk about control.

In fact, you cannot control everything around you. You cannot make your employees do the work in exactly the way you want. You cannot dictate the outcome. You cannot force your children to do their homework, eat their dinner, or dress a certain way. You may think you can, but you can't.

How many of you get upset by traffic, the weather, the service you receive at your telco provider, and the airlines? How much control do you have over them? None. Guess what? You don't have control over your spouse, partner, kids, parents, siblings, co-workers, or bosses either.

The only person you can control is you. You have absolute control over your thoughts and your behaviours. You can control how you react to events and people around you. You control the choices you make.

This means you can have your life the way you want it whether the world crumbles around you or not. You can handle it—whatever comes your way.

Let's take a closer look at the difference between controlling other people, and controlling yourself.

Controlling parent: Do your homework. Go upstairs to your bedroom and do it now. I'll be up in an hour to make sure it's done, and I'd better not see you fooling around on the Internet. Oh, by the way, I got an A in math when I was a high school student, so I can help you with those calculations.

Parent with self-control: Do you have any tests or essays due tomorrow? I'll be here in the living room if you need any help. No? That's fine. It's great to see you working so independently.

The controlling parent thinks she can force a child to do homework. The fact is, no one can force a child to read the text or do the calculations. This will only lead to a power struggle and a blow-up. It also sends a subtle message: You are not competent so I have to do it for you. Is that what you really want to tell your child?

The parent with self-control, on the other hand, makes it clear that the child is responsible for performing well at school. She's there to encourage, if necessary, but she doesn't try to step in. If the child doesn't do the homework and fails the test, she is confident the child can learn from his mistakes. The message? The child is able to do it, and the parent is there to encourage, but not interfere.

> **Controlling boss:** The controlling boss is a micro-manager, one who doesn't trust his employees to do the job and gets involved in tasks below her level. The supervisor doesn't appreciate her employees. She has high expectations and never seems satisfied.

> **Boss with self-control:** The boss with self-control knows where and when to get involved. She gives employees space to succeed or fail and sees failure as a way for people to learn. For employees to take charge, they must believe that if they don't succeed, they will still have a job.

A controlling boss removes or hinders an employee's freedom in the workplace, and along the way he creates an organization of unhappy robots who are not creating but only executing. A controlled boss understands people need to be free to discover, even if it doesn't turn out well.

Some people think they can control others, yet in the process of trying to control other people or the situation, they lose power and, ultimately, control. When someone doesn't act the way they want them to, or life doesn't go the way they want or expect, they are disappointed, angry, frustrated, resentful. When these emotions come into play, it's a pretty clear sign of a loss of power.

Some control freaks try to be more subtle. They attempt to manipulate or coerce people into doing what they want. One of my clients played this game. She told employees to come into her office with new ideas. But she was a perfectionist, a controlling person, and the only ideas she genuinely liked were hers. So not surprisingly, she always ended up shooting down her employees' ideas.

Her open-door policy backfired. The staff quickly got the message and stopped coming into her office. Creativity sank like a stone. They resigned themselves to doing what they were told. Productivity went down, and she couldn't understand why. The reason was simple: If you have a controlling type at the top, innovation gets squashed. But if you have a controlling type pretending not to be one, then the employees won't invest themselves into the job, and engagement will flounder.

Having control over your life and controlling other people in your life are very different. Having control over your life is one of the basic principles of this book. It means you take responsibility for your actions and reactions, and how you view anything that happens to you. It means making choices, after looking at multiple options, so that you can live in a place of personal power and control.

Feeling in control of your life is a key component to happiness. Trying to control others is very different. You could end up being very frustrated because you do not, in the end, control the outcome.

Here I Am. Now Make Me Happy

I have a few clients who ask the same thing: "Are there are no good men in this town?" It may sound silly in a large city, given that some of the male residents must be single and friendly. Yet you can hear single women of a certain age ask this all the time. It's very revealing—not of the men in their town, but of them.

What they're actually saying is this: Someone else is responsible for a key part of my happiness, which is finding a mate. So these women wait for Mr. Right to come along and deliver them from an unhappy place. In doing so, they've given away their power and their control over their happiness to Mr. Right. Then, if they meet him at a party, they wait for the call. Then, if they do go out on a date, they wait for the next call, and if he doesn't call in three days, they start badgering their friends about how long they should wait before they give up. What we're seeing is all reaction. There's no power in that waiting. On the contrary, waiting by the phone makes her feel anxious, twitchy. She wonders whether she's attractive enough for the guy. She starts feeling low, and the next Saturday night is shaping up as another remote-control night with toast and peanut butter.

You might think you only have partial control over your dating life—after all, it takes two to tango, right? You might think you have only a 50% share in the partnership at home or in your work life.

Yet you will gain tremendous power if you try out this audacious proposal: Take 100% responsibility, even if there is another person (the spouse, the date, the boss, the employee) involved. This means taking 100% of the responsibility for how the relationship is going. If you take only 50%, you are giving someone else half of the control over your happiness.

Take my client waiting for Mr. Right. What if she decides to take 100% responsibility for herself? She could make the calls to set up a date or another date. She could actually choose whom she wants to see on a Saturday night, instead of waiting to be chosen. She'd be more authentic and more powerful as a result. Maybe he'd say no, but at least she'd be in the driver's seat and could find someone else to see on Saturday night instead of sitting at home, waiting.

Here's another example. I have a client who loves flowers. She loves getting flowers sent to her, and particularly she loves her husband coming home with flowers in his hand—she just loves everything about flowers. When she first started dating her husband, she waited for him to bring her flowers. She told him how much she loved them and that when they came from him, it was even better. Once in a while he would come home with flowers or send them on Valentine's Day, but other than that, it just seemed to slip his mind. One day as she complained about his lack of caring because he didn't bring her flowers, I suggested she take 100% responsibility for this. Perplexed, she asked what that meant. If it was flowers she wanted, I said, she should take responsibility for making that happen. So she put it in his schedule: once a month flowers were to be delivered to her. She also treated herself to flowers once a week. Then one day, flowers arrived as a surprise, delivered by her husband. It was a wonderful bonus. She has kept up these types of acts, taking complete responsibility for many other areas of her marriage in addition to the flowers.

Remember the vice-president of finance who complained she never had time? She was besieged by employees who wanted her to solve their routine problems, so she didn't have time to do her own work because she was helping everyone else. She realized that her constant complaints were only making her frustrated, so I asked her why she was doing this. It started with her basic beliefs: She was the kind of person who thinks that if you want to do something, do it yourself. She was also a committed employee who wanted to do everything she could to make the company great.

Here was the key. She had to see that doing minor tasks for other people wasn't making the company great. She would deliver far more value to the company if she concentrated on her own job as controller, rather than fixing other people's problems.

She acknowledged that right away. She took 100% responsibility for her job. She spoke with the managers of the employees who used to file into her office. From now on, she said, the employees needed to figure out their problems on their own or go to their own managers for help, not her. She stuck to her guns. When employees now came into her office with a problem, she sent them away to handle it.

One week later, she was amazed how much time she had for her work. She was happy now because she now realized she could say yes or no.

This is what the 100% rule means: It's your job to make your life great, to fulfill your dreams. You're not responsible for everything that happens to you, but you can be 100% responsible for how you react and what you will do about it. Will you let external circumstances bring you down? Or will you take charge and move forward?

Fear—What Are You Afraid Of?

"I can't" often means you are afraid of something. You're afraid of failing, afraid of what people will think and say, afraid of how they'll react, afraid of the unknown, afraid of the future.

Altering who you are is scary. Going outside your comfort zone is scary.

You're not going to do it well the first couple of times because it's new.

Why is it that moving from either the safety position of being stuck or from the victim zone is scary? Is it because you have to take responsibility for the changes success or failure bring? You can't blame anyone else. You have to do something you have never done and, in the process, get uncomfortable. It's human nature to default to a position of doing nothing rather than trying.

Once you start this journey, you might find that friends and family want you to stay the way you are. When you try to stand up for yourself and take on personal power, you might even get negative feedback. They aren't used to you being powerful or interacting with you in a new way as it involves their needing to change. When you make changes and are different, you will cause other people to treat you differently. Sometimes it's a good thing: Your kids start listening, or your spouse starts paying more attention, or your boss starts giving you more responsibility. But for others in your world, this difference in you might be unnerving. They can no longer be the same with you. They might not like it.

Sure, it's scary to venture into a new world. But ask yourself right now: What is your current modus operandi getting you? How is it working for you? Are you getting what you want? Are you happy? Is it worth it?

If you don't change, what are you going to say to yourself 20 years from now? What will you say to yourself if you look back at this period, when you were stuck and unhappy, and you wonder why you didn't do anything?

It's normal to be scared when you're contemplating a big change in how you approach life. The question is what action you will take when facing your fear.

Fear has many faces. It can hide underneath something else. *How do I live without him?* Perhaps what you really fear is living alone. Or you're afraid that you won't find anyone else to love. Perhaps you are afraid that if you leave and discover you miss your partner, there will be no chance to repair the split.

I can't speak up because I'll lose my job. Fear lurks underneath those words. You think you won't find another job because you have created an internal dialogue that says you're not smart enough or good enough.

If I say what I think, they won't like me. You're afraid you're not worth it, so you become what you think other people want you to be.

These fearful statements point to deeply held beliefs about yourself. Now that you can see those beliefs, you can examine them and change them. Look at the belief. Expose it to the sunlight of reason. Is it true today? Notice how this belief sparks negative feelings. Can you name them? Can you see how that belief and those feelings give rise to the fearful statement you just expressed?

Now recommit to who you want to be. Visualize that person, and affirm it throughout the day.

You can practise combatting your fear by starting small, in a safe place. A friend of mine was scared to go to the gym. She was scared people would look at her and judge her or that she would look out of place in the classes and do the exercises incorrectly. She desperately wanted to work out, lose weight, and get into shape but had been afraid to put herself out there by going to the gym. We discussed many options for her to get past her fears. She could hire a trainer. She could go with a friend, she could go at off hours, she could just participate in the classes she knew she could do. In the end she realized that her fear, not her, was running the show. So she chose to take a small step to move past that fear and not let it dominate her. She decided to go to the gym with a friend during peak hours, and on the occasions her friend could not go, she would go to classes that were held during off hours when fewer people were there.

You too can take a small step: Ask someone—such as a friend or a potential love interest—out for coffee. Show affection to a loved one whom you have neglected for a while. Go to a job interview without quitting your old job. Take the interview even if it only amounts to practice. Do something to push yourself physically or mentally. Do something you would not normally do, something outside your comfort zone.

Change can be scary because we don't know what is on the other side. Who would we be if we didn't do what we always do? How would we get along with others if we changed? Might we lose friends or family members? But the more we face the unknown, the less frightening it becomes. And the more risks you take, the easier they look. The further outside your comfort zone you go, the wider that zone gets. What was scary yesterday is today's normal. By taking baby steps, you can tiptoe into the new zone and find your footing.

I'm Doing It for the Kids, My Parents, the Church ...

I'm doing it for the kids. Who can argue with that? It's selfless, isn't it? Surely this is far more noble than thinking of what makes you happy and fulfilled.

Most of us were raised to think of others before ourselves. And somehow, for many, this turns into a life. If you always think about others before yourself, and you don't make decisions based on what makes you feel happy and fulfilled, where will you be?

You'll be resentful, regretful. You'll make the kids feel guilty because you sacrificed your own happiness and success for them. How do you think that will affect them?

I can't go back to work full-time because I don't want my kids to be brought up by someone else. This is another version of the same line. It seems selfless, but look at the result: You had a career before, and now you're a reluctant housewife. Your sense of obligation makes it feel as if this isn't your choice. So you feel constrained, unimportant, or marginalized. You're powerless, angry, and resentful of friends who are still in the workforce. You blame your husband because you lost your career and part of your independence. You make others feel guilty. You're stuck and resentful because you're doing something out of a good intention that you realize you no longer want to do. Why? Because of the kids.

There is nothing wrong with staying home with the kids, or staying in a marriage or on a job because of the kids. But make a powerful choice about it. You can say: *I would like my children to have two parents until they're grown up, so I'm staying.* Here you are making a clear choice to put others ahead of yourself. It's powerful.

That's very different from saying, *I'm doing it for the kids,* which suggests you have no say and no power. Abdicating power will only make you resentful and angry. If you're in that place, ask yourself what kind of spouse and mother and friend and workmate you can be. In time the anger will infect your most precious relationships.

While you would typically be advised to grin and bear it, when you're angry, you become preoccupied with your thoughts, and you're not focusing on other people, including your children. You're constantly thinking about your problems. That well of anger inside is just waiting to spill out when the right moment presents itself. The littlest things set you off.

Don't hide behind the guilt trip implicit in the words "I'm doing it for the kids." You have just handed responsibility for your happiness to your kids. You are the only one saying it. You can go back to work and send your children to daycare. You can leave your job or even your marriage if you choose to. Or you can choose not to. Just be clear about the choice. The power is knowing you have a choice and being responsible for the choices you have, as they are yours and only yours. You might not have great options, but you always have choices.

We expect to be happy, and there's nothing wrong with wanting it. If you choose to honour an obligation that you feel is important over your personal happiness, that's a powerful choice. You are taking responsibility for how your life is going. You accept the outcome of your choice. You may not be 100% happy, but you'll be happier than you would be if you felt you were stuck with a lousy deal.

The Ultimate Trap: The Victim Mindset

When I discussed being a victim earlier, my examples all had to do with specific circumstances. In other words, they all involved someone struggling with an event or a particular dilemma in which they felt powerless and were taking little or no responsibility for coming up with choices. Most of us think or act like victims once in a while or in one or two areas of our lives. But those with a victim mindset take it to the next level: They approach every part of their lives blaming others and shrugging off their responsibility. They also harbour plenty of bitterness and resentment and feel a great deal of self-pity. What's more, they seem particularly attached to this position. It's how they think of themselves—*I'm always the victim.*

This is of course a bad place to be. As a victim, you have no power. You have no say over what happens to you. You are at the mercy of your circumstances, because you can't see any way to change your situation. And if you approach everything you do with this mindset, you don't have much chance of being happy.

To be clear, dreadful things, incidents well beyond someone's control, do happen to people. Abuse, accidents, or being dealt a terrible hand happens. Failing health for all of us is a fact of life. And I am certainly not blaming those who are victims of acts of violence or terrible accidents. If you were assaulted or were hit by a drunk driver, it's obviously not your fault. If you lost your home to a tornado or your livelihood to an industry collapse, there is nothing you can do about what happened.

But none of these traumatic events have to become your identity. In most cases, you can choose how you will react and what you will do, even if you did nothing to invite the bad stuff that rained down on you.

Those with a victim mindset don't do this. Instead of taking charge of their reactions, they make excuses and blame other people for the way they turned out. *If my brother hadn't bullied me when I was a child, I would have developed better self-esteem, and I would have been more successful. If my parents had ..., if my parents had not ... if ... if ...*

The victim mindset leaves a person stuck in the past, nursing old wounds, telling the same story of woe over and over again. You can meet these victims years later, and find they're still suffering from the fate they were experiencing the last time you saw them. They may claim to want to change, but they never do because at some level being a victim is who they are.

(Some victims up the ante and become martyrs. They're the ones who let people know how badly they're being treated. They seem to thrive on the attention they get for their misfortunes. They may also resort to badgering, nagging, scolding, threatening, belittling, antagonizing, and ver-bally putting down those whom they perceive to be taking advantage of them.)

In other words, it's bad enough to lose your job, watch your invest-ments collapse, lose the use of your legs, or suffer chronic pain from a sports injury. But if you let these traumas define you, and accept that these events are just a reflection of who you are, you have adopted the victim mindset. And this is a trap that will prevent you from achieving happiness and success.

Over the years, clients trapped in the victim mindset have used lines like this to absolve them of responsibility for how their lives are now:

I always attract losers in my life!
It's my parents' fault that I am the way I am.
I was bullied as a child so ...
Everyone is out to get me!
It's all in the genes ...
That's the way it is for people like me.
I can't change.
I have no luck.
I don't ...
I can't ...
I always ...
This sucks!

Try reading these statements out loud. If you were that person, how would you feel?

Here are some of the telltale signs of a victim mindset. You

- Feel helpless, powerless, and out of control.
- Indulge in self-pity, or seek pity from others.

- Ask yourself, *Why me?* Or think, *Life isn't fair.*
- Justify and/or rationalize what's not right in your life.
- Blame people and/or events for what's not right in your life.
- Make yourself out to be a martyr.
- Feel angry, hostile, afraid, resentful, frustrated, and full of self-doubt.

I mentioned earlier we choose to be where we are. We might not have chosen the circumstances—the mean boss, the ski accident, the car crash—but we chose how we are reacting to it. Even if we don't think we're making a choice, we are, and it's often based on our perception of the facts, which is only our highly coloured version of what actually happened.

If this is true, why would any rational person want to feel this way? There's a benefit: When you're a victim, you get to feel sorry for yourself. You may even feel better about yourself, in the short term. After all, it wasn't your fault and there's nothing you can do. What's more, it's safe. You never have to put yourself on the line. You never have to face the uncertainty that comes with trying something unfamiliar or risky.

It also gives you an emotionally safe way of explaining to yourself and to others why your life isn't working. After all, if you were responsible for your own shortcomings, inadequacies, and failures, it might suggest there's something wrong with you, or that you're not good enough in some way. So isn't it easier to shift the blame somewhere else? That's what the blame, an excuse, or a rationalization are all about. They're about trying to preserve your ego and your sense of worth. You don't have to question yourself and face your fears, and you'll get plenty of support for this position from people around you.

The one thing you won't get is a way out of your dilemma. If you play the victim, you have abdicated power, and you are now saying to yourself that there's nothing you can do. In his book *Learned Optimism*, psychologist Dr. Martin Seligman puts it this way: "If you have a victim mentality, then you don't perceive the ability to choose. You don't recognize the direct consequences of choices you've made. Nor do you recognize new choices you could make that would take your life in a new direction. You focus on what you can't control, rather than what you can. Your experience of life is what happens to you, as opposed to what you consciously want it to be."

When you play the victim, you expect others to come to your rescue. You are shutting yourself off from the tremendous power you have to make a difference. You are creating a box for yourself, a box that will limit your opportunities and even limit what you see as possibilities for yourself, and putting your whole life into the hands of someone or something else.

How Do You Get Out of the Victim Mindset?

One of my clients came to me because she was having some trouble in her job. She was approaching the situation like a victim, blaming her boss, her co-workers, and the business environment she worked in. But I hadn't been working with her for very long when she started to complain about how hard her divorce had been on her, how it had created problems with her children, with her family, and with her friends. She thought it was particularly unfair that she had to deal with all of that since she had been raised by a single mom in difficult circumstances and had worked so hard to put herself through school and launch a career.

There was no doubt about it—my client had had her share of tough times. And she was right—life is unfair. But the more I talked with her, the clearer it became that she was caught in the victim mindset. In any given situation, in almost every aspect of her life, she felt that the odds were against her and that everyone else held all the power. It wasn't an easy conversation, but I pointed out to her that maybe she was feeling powerless and frustrated about a lot more than her job. We worked on moving her from victim to power player in her work world, but I also suggested that she apply the new tools and techniques I taught her to her family life, her friendships, and her future. And I told her that it would take time, but the results would be worth it.

Essentially, all of the power tools, exercises, story changes, and attitude adjustments that I've suggested in this book are the techniques you need to use to pull yourself out of the Victim Mindset Trap. The first step is, of course, "The YOU Factor," putting yourself back into the narrative of your life. Once you are prepared to do that, you are probably going to have to spend a lot of time examining your personal values, your personal truths and assumptions, and your stories. You are going to have to practise looking at your life and your choices from a lot of different perspectives. And in all aspects of your life, you are going to have to pay attention to how you react and to work on regaining your power and taking control.

Moving out of the Victim Mindset Trap is not a quick process, and if you lived with the mindset for a very long time, you may have to be on guard that you don't slip back for years to come. But you can do it, and you can create a happier, more fulfilling future for yourself.

Exercise: Getting out of the victim mindset

Think of the people in your life who cause you any stress or anxiety. Who is responsible for having them in your life?

You may not be happy with the people surrounding you, yet you are attracted to them and you are keeping them there. If you got into a bad relationship, who got you there? No one marched you into the relationship and kept you there at gunpoint.

You ended up there by your own free will. It was your choice. If you're not happy, it's up to you to do something about it.

And if you're not willing to do something about it, do you have the moral authority to complain?

Look at your job. Are you happy with how much money you're making? Are you happy with your level or responsibility and your activities each day? If not, you need to accept that you're completely responsible for every aspect of your job and your career. Why? Because you chose it. You took the job, you assumed the responsibilities, and you accepted the wage. If you're not happy with any of it, it's up to you to do something different.

Life tends to serve us up exactly what we put up with. If you're not happy, look around you, at people who are doing the kind of work you would like to do, or people who are living the life you would like to live. Ask what they're doing differently. How did they get what they got? Once you know, accept responsibility for your situation. Start by asking this key question: *Do I have power now? Or am I being guided by circumstances or other people?*

Look at each part of your life that you are complaining about or feel like you have no power or control over. Make a list of your problems and work each one through the power tools until you have found your power.

5

Putting "The YOU Factor" to Work

To take control of your life and your happiness, you have to be a "power player." Not coincidentally, that name implies action. Nothing changes unless you do something.

So you need to get moving.

You can read this book and learn about the power tools, but unless you use them they won't make a difference in your life. Talking about dieting and what you will do to lose weight is great, but nothing will happen unless you make your new eating habits an everyday practice. What if you just want to change the way you think or behave? Going to therapy, reading books, watching inspiring videos, journaling, practising, these are all actions directed at changing the way you think, act, or react.

No Escape Hatches

But how do you keep moving forward? Once you've changed your thinking and surveyed your options, you'll probably discover at least one concrete thing you want to do.

Whatever you choose, you are responsible for making your choice work out for you, so be 100% committed to making it work. Do not give yourself an escape hatch.

Eliminate from your vocabulary the following phrase: *If it doesn't work, I can always ...*

Don't let yourself be held back by anything. Just do it.

Here's a tip to get started: Wake up 10 minutes earlier than normal. Lie in bed. Think about what you want to change. Review the actions you're going to do that day to implement the change—and put it into your calendar. Or make a timeline for the changes and keep track of your progress.

Commitment is not about waiting for your job to get better, or your spouse to say "I love you," or your brain to motivate you to work out, or your thoughts to change. Commitment is about declaration and action. You declare what you are committed to no matter what. Committed to the point where you are putting 100% of the effort into whatever you are doing regardless of your inner voice, your feelings, or someone else's actions. (Unless of course those actions are illegal, immoral, or endangering you.) This doesn't mean you have to stay committed to someone who treats you poorly or a boss who underpays you. These cases have to be put to the test of your own value system.

Be Accountable

If you have any doubts that you will follow through with your plans, get a coach to make you accountable. That's why Weight Watchers works—it requires you to report in at regular intervals. But it doesn't have to be a coach you pay. If you've decided to run a half marathon in six months, you can get yourself a running partner. It's unlikely you will leave a friend standing on the corner at 7:30 a.m.

My husband came up with a smart idea. He was training for a gruelling race in the Gobi Desert, and his buddy wanted to run to lose weight. The deal was that they had to run 40 kilometres per week between the two of them. They'd check in with each other every Sunday and disclose the number of kilometres they had run. If the total number didn't add up to 40, the man who ran the fewest kilometres that week would have to run the unrun kilometres the next week. It worked for both of them.

The point is this: You can't do this alone. You are creating new patterns for yourself, new habits, and it takes effort and practice every day, over a long time. Even if you don't opt to work with a partner or a coach, you can create a support system by telling people about your plans—in writing or in person. Then ask them to point out to you when you are not behaving in line with the desired changes.

And don't forget to be a support to yourself. Sometimes all you need is to practise the positive stories and personal truths you already have and those you have been developing. These repeated affirmations can move you from a place of insecurity to loving and accepting yourself. Speaking to yourself in the mirror or saying these positive affirmations to yourself many times a day will rewire your brain for long-term benefits. Learning to love yourself may look difficult, but this you can do on your own!

And keep in mind, it's normal to stumble when you're trying something new, so don't expect to master it right away.

You'll fall. But when you do, don't return to the victim mentality that made you stuck and unhappy in the first place. Instead, acknowledge that the same old habit—indulging in chocolate chip cookies, bagels, or wine, for example—happened again. But remember too that that was yesterday, the past, and you can't do anything about it. Beating yourself up won't help. Starving yourself today to make up for the chocolate cake and wine of the weekend will only make you feel worse. It will steer you right back to the negative brain pattern that led you to overeat initially.

Instead, focus on how you want to be today. Acknowledge that new ways of living take practice, like learning a new golf swing or how to play guitar. Recommit to who and how you want to be in the present and the future. And always remember "The YOU Factor," the most important element in leading your happy life.

10
POWER TOOL

Power Tool 10: Put It into Action

As Nike says, "JUST DO IT." One thing you can be sure of: You won't get any results if you don't act.

One of the biggest mistakes people make is that they believe that a good intention + an excuse = result. This is, in fact, untrue. Intentions are not actions, excuses are not actions, therefore, there can be no result. An action is measurable. Imagine there is a fly on the wall and it's going to relay the message of what you did. What will it say? A fly can't see your thoughts, or your intentions, or your excuses. It only sees what you do. It sees only action. And don't confuse the action with the result you are looking for. Here's an example of someone whose good intention is to lose weight:

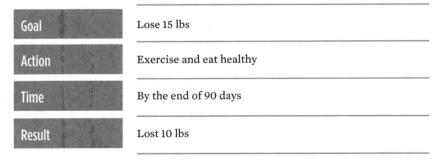

Goal	Lose 15 lbs
Action	Exercise and eat healthy
Time	By the end of 90 days
Result	Lost 10 lbs

A blank form to use for **Power Tool 10: Put It into Action** is found in the Appendix, on page 155.

Write down your goals. Make an action plan. Goals are specific, measurable, achievable, realistic, and within a specific time. Put the steps for your action plan in your calendar and stick to the plan.

Give yourself deadlines.

Measure your results.

If you need outside help, get it. Many of us need outside help for some parts of our life, like doing weights in the gym.

Put it out there. Tell your friends and colleagues. If someone else knows what you want to do, it will reinforce your change.

Their support can push you through in the tough times.

Make your goals audacious. Make them big. Make them powerful. You have read this book to gain power, be happy, and put you out front, so put your entire life into action—POWERFULLY!

You may never know what results come of your action, but if you do
nothing, there will be no result.
—Mahatma Gandhi

Conclusion

"The YOU Factor" doesn't come naturally to many of us. Sometimes that's because you honestly think you are being the best person you can be by focusing on others. But if you aren't happy, you can't truly accommodate your loved ones and the others in your life. And if your unhappiness is making you feel like a victim, then despite all of your protests that you are doing so much for others, you are really spending a lot of time looking at how they are affecting you instead of what you can do to change things.

Putting "The YOU Factor" back into your life will allow you to share the best of yourself with those around you. You will be more honest about what you need, what fills you up, what matters. You'll be clear about the activities and the people who drain you of joy. You'll be able to see the gap between your values and the way you are living right now.

In *The YOU Factor*, I have tried to make the case that many women live lives that are not as happy and fulfilled as they could be because they give away power to other people or circumstances. This book is about regaining that power, by taking responsibility and seeing that you always have a choice. Even if you can't change the circumstances, you can choose how to perceive them, and how to react. To be able to do this, you have to be aware of how you look at your life and why you tell the stories you do. What deep-set personal truths are driving your stories? It's amazing what happens once you can spot these truths and the stories you tell as a result. Once you can see them, you realize that the story you're telling is just a story—it's quite different from the known facts.

This insight will open up many more options in your personal life and your work. The barriers that you thought were fencing you in turned out to be barriers of your own making. They're stories you tell, not the hard reality out there. Now you can take down those barriers, and give yourself far more leeway to manoeuvre than you thought possible.

This might change your life, or you might decide to stay where you are. Even if you do, you'll gain a new way of looking at your world. Just knowing you have a choice can make all the difference. Knowing this will move you from that 6 out of 10. You may not hit a 10 right away but you will be on the right path for that to happen.

We all like stories with a happy ending, but the end of this story is something I cannot predict. There's no instant recipe for pure love and happiness and fulfillment at home and at work, and you won't find one here. Yet if you use the tools in this book, and keep practising them, I can assure you that your journey will be more exciting and fulfilling than it is right now. For one thing, you will be the protagonist of your own story. You will be able to take action and find ways to live and work that fulfill you and give you joy. You will not be stuck in a never-ending round of complaints that seem to trap you, year after year. Your new story won't be about them—it will be about you.

POWER TOOLS

Power Tool 1: Accept responsibility

Power Tool 2: Check your story

Power Tool 3: Look at your belief system and personal truths

Power Tool 4: Challenge your assumptions

Power Tool 5: View it from a different perspective

Power Tool 6: Know you always have a choice

Power Tool 7: Affirm yourself in a positive way—every day

Power Tool 8: Forgive, learn your lesson, and move on

Power Tool 9: Don't tolerate. Accept

Power Tool 10: Put it into action

APPENDIX
POWER TOOL
TEMPLATES

Fill-me-ups

What fills me up?	Rating	Time needed

Drains

What drains me?	Rating	Time allotment

Values and Actions

Personal value	Aligned or gap	What I did this week

Complaints

Complaint	
How long	
Rating	
Who is to blame?	
What am I getting out of it?	

Power Tool 1: Accept Responsibility

Areas in my life where I am stuck or unhappy	
Who or what is the cause of my unhappiness or complaint?	
In what ways can I take responsibility?	

Power Tool 2: Check Your Story

What's my story?	
What is my story stripped down to just the facts?	
What did I add to the facts?	

Power Tool 3: Look at Your Belief System and Personal Truths

A recurring situation that makes me react in a particular way	
What is my personal truth?	
What effect does my belief in that personal truth have on my life?	
What is the opposite truth?	
How would my situation change if I held that opposite truth?	
Should I change it?	

Power Tool 4: Challenge Your Assumptions

What's my story?	
What is my story stripped down to just the facts?	
What did I add to the facts?	
What are my assumptions about my story?	
What meaning have I given to my story based on those assumptions?	

Power Tool 5: View It from a Different Perspective

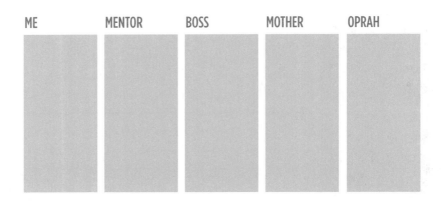

I got passed over for a promotion.

ME   MENTOR   BOSS   MOTHER   OPRAH

Changing Your Story

What's my story?

What is my personal truth?

How is it affecting me?

Is this truth worth keeping?

Power Tool 6: Know You Always Have a Choice

Situation	
Choice 1	
Choice 2	
Choice 3	
Choice 4	
Choice 5	
Choice 6	

Power Tool 7: Affirm Yourself in a Positive Way Every Day

What triggers me?	
What is the personal truth creating that reaction?	
What is the affirmation that combats that truth?	

Power Tool 8: Forgive, Learn Your Lesson, and Move On

Individuals or situations I feel are unresolved	
Emotions I am holding on to	
What do I need to forgive them or myself for?	
What is the lesson to be learned?	

Power Tool 9: Don't Tolerate. Accept

Traits of individuals in my life or my circumstances that I wish I could change	
Do I acknowledge I cannot change this?	
Declare that I accept it by either sharing it with the individual or writing it down	

Power Tool 10: Put It into Action

Goal

Action

Time

Result

Acknowledgments

One August day in 2010, I set out for a 20-kilometre run. My life was challenging at that point, and long runs were a way for me to keep my head clear. As I rounded the 10-kilometre mark, the power tools found in this book started to pop into my head. By the time I had completed the entire 20 kilometres, the concept of the book was complete. Since that time, many hours have been put in, not only by me but by others, to bring these ideas to you. It is these others I want to acknowledge here.

Thanks to my family—Stefan, Montana, and Jade. Your love, support, and understanding as I wrote instead of tending to your needs on too many occasions will forever be the greatest gift I have ever received.

Thank you as well to Sarah Scott of Barlow Book Publishing, Meg Masters, Yvonne Hunter, and Luke Despatie.